THE POWER OF CONNECTION

FROM AWKWARD TO AWESOME: BUILD SOCIAL
SKILLS, IMPROVE COMMUNICATION, BOOST
CONFIDENCE, AND CREATE LASTING
RELATIONSHIPS

LIAM GRANT

To my incredible wife,

Thank you for your unwavering love and support during my early mornings and late nights spent chasing this dream of writing and helping others. Your strength in keeping our home and family thriving has made this journey possible. I am endlessly grateful for your patience, understanding, and belief in me. Your love means the world to me, and I couldn't have done this without you.

With all my love,

Liam

CONTENTS

Introduction   9

1. FOUNDATIONS OF SOCIAL SKILLS   11
   Understanding Social Anxiety and Its Impact   12
   The Science of First Impressions   14
   Decoding Body Language Basics   16
   The Art of Active Listening   18
   The Role of Empathy in Effective Communication   20

2. NAVIGATING EVERYDAY SOCIAL
   INTERACTIONS   23
   Starting Conversations without Fear   23
   Techniques for Remembering Names and Details   25
   Small Talk: Moving beyond Weather Talks   27
   Handling Awkward Silences Gracefully   29
   Exiting Conversations Smoothly and Politely   31
   Wrapping Up Chapter 2   33

3. BUILDING CONFIDENCE AND OVERCOMING
   BARRIERS   35
   Strategies to Build Self-Confidence in Social
   Settings   35
   Overcoming the Fear of Public Speaking   38
   Dealing with Rejection in Social Contexts   40
   Transforming Negative Self-Talk in Social Scenarios   42
   Using Affirmations to Enhance Social Competence   45

4. DIGITAL COMMUNICATION IN THE SOCIAL
   MEDIA AGE   49
   Crafting Engaging Text Messages   49
   Maintaining Authenticity Online   55
   Managing Misunderstandings in Digital
   Conversations   57
   The Etiquette of Digital Disagreements   60
   Wrapping Up Digital Communication   62

5. ADVANCED COMMUNICATION SKILLS 63
Persuasion Techniques for Positive Influence 63
Negotiation Skills for Everyday Situations 67
Advanced Empathy: Connecting on a Deeper Level 70
The Power of Storytelling in Personal Connections 72
Mastering the Art of Giving and Receiving Feedback 75

6. SPECIAL SOCIAL SITUATIONS 81
Networking Like a Pro: Building Meaningful
Connections 82
First Date Conversations: Dos and Don'ts 85
Navigating Family Gatherings Successfully 88
Social Skills for Workplace Success 90
Handling Social Situations in Diverse Cultural
Contexts 93

7. DEVELOPING RELATIONSHIPS 97
Deepening Friendships: Beyond Acquaintances 97
Strategies for Long-Distance Relationships 100
Fostering Trust and Honesty in Relationships 103
Balancing Professional and Personal Relationships 105
Leading into the Next Chapter 109

8. CONFLICT RESOLUTION AND DIFFICULT
CONVERSATIONS 111
Essentials of Conflict Resolution 112
Strategies for De-escalating Tense Situations 114
Communicating during Emotional Upheavals 116
Assertiveness without Aggressiveness 118
Navigating Criticism and Negative Feedback 120
Wrapping Up Chapter 8 122

9. ENHANCING EMOTIONAL INTELLIGENCE 123
The Basics of Emotional Intelligence 123
Recognizing Emotional Triggers in Social
Interactions 126
Emotional Regulation Techniques 128
Empathy in Action: Practical Scenarios 130
Building Emotional Resilience 132

10. MAINTAINING SOCIAL SKILLS OVER TIME   137
    Lifelong Social Skills: Adapting and Growing   137
    Teaching Social Skills to Others   139
    Reflecting on Social Growth and Setting Future
    Goals   141

    Conclusion   145
    References   151
    About the Author & Upcoming Projects   155

INTRODUCTION

Have you ever felt like you're on the outside looking in during social gatherings? Or stumbled through a conversation feeling you can't find the right words? You're not alone, and I've been there, too. That's precisely why I wrote *The Power of Connection.* This book is your roadmap to navigating the intricate world of social interactions easily and confidently.

From personal experience, I know the sting of social awkwardness all too well. During my teenage years, I often blushed and stammered, barely able to muster the courage to speak up in groups. It wasn't just painful; it felt crippling. Although I got slightly better, this followed me into my adult years, causing issues with friends, work, and even my love life. Determined to change, I embarked on a journey of self-improvement, devouring every piece of advice I could find. But what truly made a difference was realizing that mastering social skills could actually be enjoyable. This revelation is at the heart of this book. I want to share with you the strategies that transformed my social life and the joy and laughter that came with learning them.

The Power of Connection isn't your typical guide filled with rigid rules. If you've ever felt like self-help books read more like dry lectures from a burnt-out professor, you're in for a pleasant surprise. This book is different. Instead, it blends humor with practical advice to make learning the ropes of effective communication genuinely fun. Think of this book as a conversation with a friend who has been in your shoes and knows exactly how to help. We'll explore everything from the basics of making a great first impression to handling complex emotional nuances in relationships.

Designed for both teens and adults, this book acknowledges that whether you are just starting high school, entering the workforce, or anywhere in between, the principles of good communication are universal. Each chapter builds on the last, forming a comprehensive journey through different facets of social interaction. You'll find plenty of real-life examples, practical exercises, and reflection prompts to help you put what you learn into practice.

Rest assured, the advice in these pages is rooted in reputable psychological research and enriched by my own experiences and those of countless others who have successfully navigated their social worlds using these methods. So, whether you want to break free from shyness, enhance your conversational skills, or deepen your relationships, this guide is your first step toward a more confident and connected life.

As we turn the page on this introduction, I invite you to dive in with an open mind and a willing heart. Embrace the exercises, reflect on the examples, and allow yourself to transform. Social mastery might seem daunting, but it's within your reach with the right tools and a bit of humor. Let's start this journey together, and by the end, I hope you'll not only master social skills but also discover a happier, more fulfilling life. Ready? Let's get started!

CHAPTER 1

FOUNDATIONS OF SOCIAL SKILLS

E ver walked into a room and felt like you were carrying a neon sign that says, "Awkward Alert!" Or maybe you've spent a whole party counting the tiles on the floor to avoid actual human interaction. Well, you're not signing up to become a professional floor-tile counter, are you? Let's put those days behind you. Welcome to the foundational course of your social skills degree—no textbooks required, just a willingness to change the script of your social life.

Social skills aren't just about chattering away at parties or networking like a boss. They start with understanding the nuts and bolts of what makes social interactions tick or, in some cases, collapse. That's what we're tackling in this first chapter. We'll cover everything from the sweaty palms of social anxiety to the heroic skills of empathy. But first, let's dive into one of the most common social gremlins and my personal weak point: social anxiety.

UNDERSTANDING SOCIAL ANXIETY AND ITS IMPACT

So, what's the deal with social anxiety? Imagine feeling a mounting sense of dread at the thought of even the most superficial social interactions—yes, even texting can bring out the cold sweats. Social anxiety isn't just about being shy or introverted. It's a persistent fear of being judged or embarrassed in social situations that can feel as crippling as showing up to a costume party ... on the wrong day.

This tricky beast can sneak up during a speech, a date, or a casual conversation with a classmate. It's like having a critical little gremlin on your shoulder, whispering not-so sweet nothings about how you might say the wrong thing. Yes, I know my Gremlin reference is aging me. Here's the kicker: this gremlin feeds on avoidance. The more you dodge social scenarios, the hungrier it gets.

But why does this happen? Well, our brains are wired to protect us from threats, and somewhere along the line, the brain can start to flag social interactions as a 'Danger Zone.' This can stem from past embarrassments, overly critical parenting, or even genetics. The result? Your body goes into a mini fight-or-flight mode. Heart races, palms sweat, and words stumble.

Impact on Social Skills

Let's talk impact. Social anxiety doesn't just keep you from enjoying parties. It can sabotage relationships, career opportunities, and personal growth. Picture avoiding a group project or a networking event because the thought alone triggers a panic spiral. Or maybe you find yourself speechless on a date, not out of awe but because your anxiety has put your vocabulary on lockdown. It's like having a brain freeze without the ice cream.

This gremlin doesn't have to rule your social life, though. Managing the symptoms is totally within reach and starts with recognizing what's happening. It's about telling yourself, "Okay, brain, I see what you're doing. Not cool."

Managing Symptoms

First up, let's dim the lights on that anxiety gremlin. Basic relaxation techniques like deep breathing or progressive muscle relaxation can be game-changers. They help reduce the physical symptoms of anxiety by telling your body, "Hey, it's okay. We're just chatting, not wrestling a lion. "Picture yourself breathing in calm and breathing out gremlins.

Next, we've got cognitive-behavioral approaches. These are like gremlin training sessions. They help you challenge and change the fearful thoughts that fuel anxiety. It's about rewriting those mental scripts that say, "I'm going to mess up," to "Hey, I can handle this." Consider editing your mental screenplay to include fewer horror scenes and more rom-com moments.

And remember mindfulness. This isn't just for yoga enthusiasts. Mindfulness helps you stay present in the moment rather than getting lost in worries about the next social event on your calendar. It teaches you to observe your thoughts and feelings without judgment, giving you a clearer headspace for handling social interactions.

Encouraging Positive Experiences

Finally, let's build some positive momentum. Gradually exposing yourself to social situations might sound about as appealing as a polar plunge in January, but it's effective. Start small—a quick chat with a barista or a hello to a neighbor. These are your training weights. Your confidence muscles grow as you rack up more positive (or even neutral) experiences.

By taking these steps, you not only reduce the anxiety volume but also set the stage for richer, more engaging social interactions. Who knows? You might even start to enjoy those parties, or at least not dread them. And that, my friend, is a victory in itself.

So, grab your metaphorical social toolkit. We're building bridges over the rivers of anxiety, making sure that the gremlin gets a lot less airtime. Ready to tackle the next social skill? Let's keep the momentum going.

THE SCIENCE OF FIRST IMPRESSIONS

Have you ever wondered why your mom told you to "dress nice and smile" before you went to that interview or why you instantly liked that one barista with funky glasses? Well, it's not just random preference; there's a whole science behind these snap decisions, which we call first impressions. It turns out our brains are pretty quick judges. Within milliseconds of meeting someone, we've already decided whether they're trustworthy, competent, or likable. This mental quick draw is all thanks to a mix of psychological phenomena, including the notorious halo effect. This is where our overall impression of a person ("Wow, they have great shoes!") bleeds into our judgments of their character ("I bet they're a great listener!"). Simplistic? Yes. Accurate? Only sometimes.

Now, why should you care? Whether it's fair or not, these first impressions stick, and they matter. I'm not saying that to scare you, but so you understand its importance.

They set the stage for future interactions and can open or close doors with others. Consider a job interview where your potential future boss is forming their first impression before you've even had a chance to dazzle them with your professional prowess. Or think about a first date, where your partner is likely assessing everything from your punctuality to your choice of shoes. These initial snapshots can influence how personal and professional relationships proceed, even if they do.

So, how do you ensure that your first impression is not just good but great? Start with the basics: body language, attire, and verbal communication. Walking into a room with a confident stride and a warm, genuine smile can work wonders. Fake it if you must. Dress appropriately for the occasion—an outfit that says, "I respect this situation and am prepared for it," can speak volumes before you even utter a hello. And when you talk, make sure your intention reflects what you're saying. Clear, articulate speech, peppered with polite, engaging questions, shows you're both interested and interesting. Bonus points if you can pull off a witty comment about the weather without sounding like a walking cliché.

But what if the first impression wasn't stellar? Maybe you spilled coffee on your shirt right before a meeting or were so nervous that you accidentally introduced yourself with the wrong name (hey, it happens!). Don't worry; first impressions aren't always the last word. Changing someone's perception takes time and consistency but is far from impossible. Consistency in your behavior is critical. Suppose you consistently show kindness, professionalism, and reliability. In that case, those qualities will start to replace any initial misgivings people might have had. It's about showing up, again and again, as the best version of yourself, letting your actions speak louder than that unfortunate coffee stain.

In essence, mastering the art of first impressions isn't just about putting on a good show once. It's about setting a standard for yourself and meeting it consistently, no matter whom you're with or where you are. Whether it's a handshake or a shared joke across a crowded room, these moments are your chance to start your story on the right foot. So next time you step into a social setting, take a deep breath, straighten your back, and remember: you're not just making a first impression. You're starting a potential new chapter with every hello. And who knows? That barista with the funky glasses may become your next best friend-or at least your go-to for coffee recommendations.

DECODING BODY LANGUAGE BASICS

Ever tried to decipher someone's poker face during a game or wondered why your best friend seemed off despite insisting they're "fine"? Welcome to the world of body language, the silent orchestra conducting much of our social interactions. It's like being a detective in your own social life, where every gesture, posture, and micro-expression holds clues to what's really going on beneath the surface.

Let's start with the basics. Body language includes the myriad of nonverbal cues we send and receive, such as facial expressions, gestures, and postures. Have you ever heard the term "resting bitch face?" I bet that's a clue we've all seen at one point or another. That's one you'll want to avoid. That's body language. For instance, crossed arms can signal defensiveness or discomfort. At the same time, a genuine smile (the one that reaches the eyes and makes them crinkle) screams, "I'm actually happy!" Understanding these cues gives you a backstage pass to what people likely feel beyond what they're saying. It's about tuning into a silent channel that's always broadcasting.

But here's the plot twist: this channel plays a different show world-wide. Cultural variations in body language are vast. A thumbs-up in one country might be a cheerful "good job," while in others, it's offensive. In many parts of Asia, avoiding direct eye contact is a sign of respect. In contrast, it's often interpreted as a lack of interest or confidence in Western cultures. Navigating this requires a bit of cultural homework to avoid miscommunication. Remember, when in Rome, do as the Romans do—or at least try not to accidentally offend them with a poorly chosen hand gesture.

How can you use body language to amp up your communication game? It's one thing to understand it; it's another to apply it effectively. Start by mirroring the body language of the person you're talking to, which can create a sense of empathy and understanding.

Notice they're leaning in? Lean in a bit, as well. It shows engagement and builds trust. But keep it natural; you don't want to look like you're playing a game of Simon Says. Also, consider your posture: standing or sitting straight (but not stiff), which exudes confidence and shows you're open to communication.

Interpreting others' body language is where your inner detective shines. Let's say you're chatting with a classmate about a group project and notice them glancing at the door. Instead of droning on, you might cut to the chase and ask if they need to be somewhere. Recognizing these subtle cues can prevent you from misreading a situation or missing out on underlying messages. It's about being observant but not obsessive. Watch people's body language, but don't stare like you're trying to see into their soul— that's just creepy.

By mastering these nonverbal nuances, you turn every interaction into an opportunity to connect more deeply and understand people beyond their words. Whether you're trying to nail a job interview, make a new friend, or get through a family dinner without a mishap, being fluent in body language can give you an edge. It's like having a superpower where you can hear what isn't said—that's some next-level social skills right there! And while it might seem daunting at first, with a bit of practice, you'll be reading the room like a pro, making each social encounter a little less puzzling. Plus, who doesn't want to feel like Sherlock Holmes, minus the deerstalker hat?

THE ART OF ACTIVE LISTENING

Imagine you're in the middle of telling a friend about the absolute worst day of your life—you're talking epic, movie-level disaster—and just as you're about to reveal the climax, they look at their phone and chuckle at a meme. Ouch, right? That sting you feel is the lack of active listening, a crucial skill that's about as underrated as a quiet drummer in a rock band. So, what exactly is active listening, and why should you care? It's not just hearing the words; it's about fully engaging with them, understanding the message, and responding thoughtfully. It's the difference between nodding and getting why your friend is obsessed with collecting rare, slightly creepy dolls.

Active listening is like a superpower in the world of communication. It involves several key components: paying full attention, withholding judgment, reflecting, and clarifying. Paying full attention means being present in the moment. There are better times to multitask, planning your dinner while someone shares their soul. It's about giving your undivided attention to the speaker, making eye contact, and not just waiting for your turn to talk. Withholding judgment is crucial because it's easy to start forming opinions before the person even finishes speaking. Keeping an open mind helps understand the context and the emotions behind the words.

Reflecting and clarifying are about ensuring you've received the message as intended. This could be as simple as saying, "So, what you're saying is…" and repeating what you think you heard. This shows that you're not only listening but also processing the information. It's like being a mirror—instead of reflecting an image, you're reflecting words and feelings. Now, you might wonder how to actually improve these skills. Techniques like paraphrasing what the speaker has said can reinforce that you understand (or highlight that you need more clarification). Asking open questions also keeps the conversation flowing. Instead of asking yes or no questions, probe a little deeper. For instance, instead of asking, "Did you like the movie?" try to ask, "What did you think about the movie's take on friendship?"

The benefits of sharpening your active listening skills stretch far beyond just making you a communication ninja. In personal relationships, it creates a deeper connection and builds trust. When people feel heard, they open up, share, and engage more. That's the type of relationship we all look for, so do your part, ask open questions, tear down those walls, and answer them fully when someone asks you. In professional settings, it can prevent misunderstandings, save time (because you're not constantly backtracking to fix miscommunications), and even boost your career. After all, bosses and colleagues tend to notice when you're the one who actually gets things done right because you are paying attention.

Active listening also lays the groundwork for resolving conflicts. By genuinely understanding all sides of a story, you're better equipped to come up with fair solutions. It's hard to stay mad at someone when you know where they're coming from. Think about it: how many arguments could have been avoided if everyone involved had just taken a moment to really listen to each other? Imagine the peace treaty possibilities if everyone mastered the art of listening!

So, stepping up your listening game is a pretty smart move if you're trying to improve your friendships, make a good impression at work, or become a better communicator. It's about making the person speaking to you feel like they're the most important person in the room. And who doesn't want to feel like that? Next time you're in a conversation, try putting your phone away; it's hard, I know, but do it, make eye contact, and focus on what's being said. You might be surprised at how much you've been missing. After all, good conversationalists are made, not born, and it starts with listening—not just hearing. So, get out there and become the boss of your social circle-one empathetic ear at a time.

THE ROLE OF EMPATHY IN EFFECTIVE COMMUNICATION

Ever tried to explain your bad day to someone, and instead of getting a "that sucks, I'm here for you," you get a "Yeah, but everyone has bad days"? That right there is the difference between empathy and sympathy. It's one thing to recognize someone's boat is sinking and entirely another to hop in and help them bail the water. That's empathy in a nutshell—it's not just understanding the emotions others are feeling but also sharing them, at least a little. And before you think it's about being a mind reader or a saint, let me tell you, it's not as mystical or saintly as it sounds; it's actually deeply rooted in our brain's wiring.

Empathy is like the emotional glue that holds human relationships together. From a psychological standpoint, it involves mirror neurons in our brain. These little guys and gals fire up not only when you perform an action but also when you see someone else doing it, allowing you to 'mirror' the emotions of others. It's why you wince when someone stubs their toe or feel happy when you see someone laughing. This mirroring helps us understand what others are feeling without them having to spell it out.

Developing empathetic skills is like tuning an instrument. It requires practice, attention, and sometimes a bit of tweaking. A great place to start is with perspective-taking. Try stepping into someone else's shoes—figuratively, of course, unless you're the same shoe size and they're cool with it. Think about their background, their day, and their stressors. What's their story? This isn't about agreeing with them all the time but about understanding where they're coming from. Practicing emotional intelligence goes hand in hand with this. It's about being aware of your emotions, managing them, and recognizing emotions in others. This can be as simple as noticing when someone seems off and asking what's up rather than ignoring it or making assumptions.

In communication, empathy can be a game changer. Imagine you're a manager, and an employee comes to you upset about a mistake they made. An empathetic response might involve:

- Acknowledging their feelings ("I see you're really upset about this").
- Expressing understanding ("It's normal to feel this way when things don't go as planned").
- Offering support ("Let's figure out the next steps together").

This approach soothes the employee and opens a pathway for constructive dialogue and problem-solving. It's about making the person feel heard and supported, which can transform a potentially explosive situation into a collaborative effort to find a solution.

But here's the real talk: I'm not here to make everything seem easy and funny. I'm also here to be truthful. Being empathetic can be challenging. It's emotionally demanding. One of the significant challenges is emotional burnout, which is like empathy fatigue. You give so much of yourself trying to be there for everyone else that you end up feeling drained. It's like every time you had a coffee with a friend, you left feeling like you'd run a marathon. Not sustainable, right? So, managing this starts with setting emotional boundaries. It's okay not to always be the shoulder to cry on. You can be supportive without taking on everyone else's emotional baggage. Self-care isn't just a trendy term; it's essential here. Regular check-ins with yourself, knowing when you need a break, and engaging in activities that replenish your energy are all crucial. So take the stewardess's advice and put on your oxygen mask before helping others.

Empathy isn't just a nice-to-have; it's the oil that keeps the engine of human interaction running smoothly. It enhances your relationships, makes you a better communicator, and can even make you a better friend, partner, or leader. So, take a moment next time you find yourself in a situation where tensions are high. Take a breath. Try to see the person in front of you and understand their feelings. It may change the entire direction of the interaction. After all, a little empathy goes a long way in a world that can be all too ready to judge and dismiss. And who knows? The next time your day goes sideways, the empathy you've shown others is what comes back to you.

CHAPTER 2
NAVIGATING EVERYDAY SOCIAL INTERACTIONS

E ver found yourself at a party clutching a solo cup with no idea how to break into the circle of people laughing about some inside joke, feeling like you're on the outside of an invisible wall? Or maybe you've been stuck in an elevator with a co-worker you've barely spoken two words to, the silence stretching out like a bad sitcom scene? You're not alone. Stepping into the realm of everyday social interactions can sometimes feel like entering a minefield blindfolded. But hey, it doesn't have to be a nerve-wracking ordeal—let's turn it into an adventure in charm and wit!

STARTING CONVERSATIONS WITHOUT FEAR

Let's tackle the big, scary monster under the bed—starting conversations. This initial hurdle can feel like jumping over a ten-foot wall for many. But what if I told you it's more like stepping over a small puddle? It's all about getting over that initial hesitation. The trick is to change the narrative in your head. Instead of telling yourself, "I'm going to sound silly," flip the script to, "What's the best that could happen?" This little tweak in mindset—from fear to curiosity—can open doors you never knew existed. Imagine the relief when you realize the monster under the bed is just a pair of mismatched socks.

Now, on to the real action: conversation openers. Forget the mundane "nice weather, huh?" unless you're chatting with a meteorologist. Tailor your opener to the setting. At a networking event? Try something like, "What brought you to this conference?" It's open-ended and shows genuine interest in the other person's story. In a casual setting, like a friend's party, you could go with something chill like, "How do you know [host's name]?" It's simple, effective, and a natural gateway into deeper conversation territories. And hey, it beats awkwardly staring at the snack table, pretending you're deeply interested in the seven-layer dip. You would be pretending; you better believe I am very interested in that dip.

Being observant plays a considerable role here. Use your environment to fuel the conversation. Is there a piece of art on the wall or a song playing that you love? Use it as a launching pad: "This song always makes me think of summer. What's your go-to summer tune?" It's relaxed, relatable, and, most importantly, natural.

But what about practice? Here's where role-playing isn't just for Dungeons & Dragons enthusiasts. Try practicing conversation starters with a friend or in a mirror. Role-play different scenarios and throw in some curveballs, like a friend acting disinterested. It's like a workout for your social muscles. The more you practice, the less daunting real interactions become. Just don't end up arguing with your reflection; that's a whole different set of issues.

Interactive Exercise: Conversation Starter Scenarios

To really flex those conversational muscles, let's try an interactive exercise. Imagine you're at three different events: a book launch (I know, a little on the nose for me). A friend's barbecue and a community workshop. For each scenario, jot down three openers you could use that are specific to the event. Think about what's unique to the setting and who you might meet. This isn't just theoretical—next time you're at a similar event, pull out one of these openers and watch the magic happen.

By changing your mindset, crafting engaging openers, being observant, and practicing, you'll turn what was once a daunting challenge into just another enjoyable part of your social toolkit. So, next time you find yourself at an event, take a deep breath, remember your training, and dive into those conversations confidently. Who knows? The next person you speak to could become a new friend, a business partner, or even a future costar in your life's adventures.

TECHNIQUES FOR REMEMBERING NAMES AND DETAILS

Ever found yourself squirming because you just called someone by the wrong name, or worse, you've drawn a complete blank in the middle of an introduction? It's like your brain decides to take a little vacation right when you need it the most. Remembering names and those little details might seem like a small part of social interactions, but boy, does it pack a punch in making or breaking your social credibility? It's not just about avoiding that awkward "Hey ... you!" moment. Knowing someone's name and recalling specifics about them can turn a generic interaction into a personal connection that feels genuine and respectful. It shows you value the person enough to keep their information in your mental Rolodex.

So, why is nailing this name game so crucial? When you remember someone's name, you're not just recognizing them but also giving them a subtle compliment. You're saying, "You mattered enough for me to remember you." This is golden in both personal and professional settings. It sets a foundation of trust and respect, paving the way for smoother interactions and deeper relationships. Whether it's a client, a colleague, or a new friend, using their name is like a secret handshake that says, "I see you." Plus, it avoids that embarrassing moment when you call Karen "Sharon" and she glares at you like you just insulted her cat.

Now, on to the how. Let's dive into some memory aids and techniques that are about to make your life a whole lot easier. Mnemonic devices are your new best friends. These are memory tricks that help you recall names and details. For example, try linking a name with a visual image. Met a Bob who has big blue eyes? Picture those "Bs"—Bob's Big Blues. It sounds silly, but the sillier it is, the better your brain can keep hold of it. Associative thinking is another handy tool. This involves creating a story or a connection between the name and something familiar to you. If Julia likes jogging, imagine her jogging in July—Julia jogs in July. And good old repetition never fails. Repetitively using the person's name in conversation helps you memorize it and makes the interaction feel more personal.

Active listening is where you turn your attention up a notch. This isn't about nodding along while planning your lunch. It's about engaging fully—listening to the words, noticing the details, and embedding them into your memory. When someone tells you about their passion for pottery or pet parrots, lock those details in. Repeat them back in your mind, and maybe even out loud: "So, making pottery is your weekend warrior activity, huh?" Using the details shows you're interested and cements them in your brain.

Lastly, let's talk about follow-up practices. Ever thought of using tech to boost your memory? Digital tools are fantastic for keeping track of the details you might otherwise forget. After meeting someone, take a minute to jot down notes on your phone or a planner. Write their name, key information from your conversation, and anything specific you want to remember. This practice is beneficial in professional settings where you meet many people simultaneously. Before the next meeting, a quick glance at your notes can refresh your memory, enabling you to confidently greet each person. "Hey, Mark! How was the fishing trip you mentioned last time?" Just watch their faces light up because you remember.

You transform routine interactions into meaningful exchanges by marrying these techniques with a genuine interest in people. It's not just about avoiding social faux pas; it's about building bridges. With names and details locked down, you're not just another face in the crowd—you're the person who makes everyone feel like a star in their own right. Remember, in the symphony of social interactions, these techniques are your instruments—play them well, and the melody of your social life will be sweeter than ever.

SMALL TALK: MOVING BEYOND WEATHER TALKS

Picture this: You're stuck in an elevator with someone you've just met, and the only thing that pops into your head is, "Nice weather we're having, huh?" Sure, it's a classic, but let's be honest, talking about the weather is the small talk equivalent of sitting on the bench in a basketball game. You're in the game, but you're not really playing. Let's amp up your game to MVP levels by expanding those small talk topics into something that not only breaks the ice but melts it completely.

First off, think about what's buzzing around. What's the latest book that's got everyone hooked, or the new series that people are binge-watching? There could be a tech gadget that's got everyone talking or a travel destination that's trending. These topics are goldmines for small talk because they're current and likely to spark interest. Imagine bumping into someone at a coffee shop and starting with, "Have you read the latest *The Power of Connection* book that's been all over the news? I heard it's a real page-turner!" It instantly shifts gears from mundane to engaging. It's all about catching that wave of what's current and riding it into the conversation.

Now, while it's great to get the ball rolling, the real magic of small talk is in transitioning it into more profound, meaningful territory. This is where you turn a casual chat into a memorable conversation. Pay close attention to how the other person responds to your topics. Are their eyes lighting up when you mention a particular movie, or do they give more than just a nod when you talk about a recent scientific discovery? These are your cues to dive deeper. Ask open-ended questions that invite them to elaborate. "What did you think about the twist at the end of that film?" or "How do you think that new tech could change our daily lives?" This shows you're not just making conversation but are genuinely interested in their thoughts and feelings. It's this genuine interest that can transform small talk from filler conversation into a bridge toward a stronger connection.

Staying informed is your secret weapon here. The more you know, the more you have to talk about. Make it a habit to skim through news headlines, check out the latest bestsellers, or even scroll through reviews of the newest gadgets. This doesn't mean you need to be an encyclopedia of information. However, having a few topical and varied interests can make you a versatile conversationalist. Imagine shifting from discussing the latest Oscar-winning movie to sharing insights on a recent scientific breakthrough. It makes you interesting and shows you're engaged with the world around you. This is a great way to avoid those awkward silences where you're both just staring at your feet.

Lastly, always be mindful of the other person's interests. This isn't just about showcasing your ability to chat about various topics. It's about creating a two-way street of dialogue. Watch for cues that they might be less interested in a topic—maybe they're giving short answers or their attention is drifting. That's your sign to switch gears. Maybe move from discussing international politics to something lighter, like travel aspirations. It's like being a DJ at a party; when you notice the dance floor isn't feeling the vibe, you switch up the track. The goal is to keep the energy of the conversation lively and engaging.

By broadening your small talk topics, showing genuine interest in deepening the conversation, staying informed, and being attuned to the other person's engagement, you turn every small talk opportunity into a doorway to richer, more engaging connections. So next time you reach for the "nice weather" remark, remember, you have a whole arsenal of interesting topics just waiting to make that conversation not just good but great.

HANDLING AWKWARD SILENCES GRACEFULLY

Ever found yourself in the middle of a chat, and suddenly, it's like the mute button got hit? There you are, stuck in a silence so thick you could cut it with a knife. But before you start panicking or plotting your nearest exit strategy, let's spin this around. These moments of silence? They're not the conversation killers we often make them out to be. In fact, they can be your secret weapon in mastering the art of chatting. It's all about embracing the pause, not fearing it.

First up, let's normalize the silence. Think of it this way: conversations are like music, and just as in music, where a rest note gives depth and emotion to a melody, a pause in a conversation can add weight and significance to what's being said. It's natural. It's normal. It's a pause, not a complete stop. When you start viewing these silences as natural parts of a conversation's rhythm, they become less intimidating and more of an opportunity. It's about learning to be comfortable in that quiet space, not just for you but for the other person. This mutual comfort can only come from understanding that thinking, reflecting, and breathing are okay before diving back in.

Now, let's talk strategy—using these pauses effectively. A pause can be a perfect moment to gather your thoughts and consider what's been said. It allows you a beat to think about how to reply thoughtfully or to decide the direction in which you want the conversation to go. Use this time to reflect on the discussion points, and when you reenter the conversation, you can do so with clarity and purpose. This doesn't just keep the chat flowing; it shows you're engaged and value what's being discussed. Plus, a well-timed pause before delivering a point can make what you say next seem even more insightful. It's like using a highlighter in a book—you're drawing attention right where it's needed.

But what about when a pause feels like it's dragging on a bit too long? Here's where you can gently steer the ship back on course. This is not about filling space with just anything but mindfully choosing a way to reconnect. You can circle back to something previously mentioned that perhaps sparked interest. "You mentioned earlier that you love hiking. Have you found any interesting trails around here recently?" This jumps back into familiar waters and shows you are paying attention. Or, why not introduce a new, related topic? "Speaking of movies, have you seen any good ones lately?" Finding that thread to reconnect can smoothly transition you back into comfortable dialogue.

And if you find yourself stuck, remember that humor and anecdotes are your lifelines. Injecting a light, funny remark or a relevant short story can bridge the gap between awkward silence and flowing conversation. "This silence reminded me of a funny thing that happened the other day ..." It's casual, easy, and often invites a smile or a laugh, breaking the tension and warming things back up. The key here is to keep it light and relatable; your goal is to ease the moment, not overshadow it.

Handling awkward silences with grace isn't about fearing them but embracing them as natural parts of any conversation. It's about using these moments to enhance the dialogue, reflect on the exchange, and find meaningful ways to continue the interaction. By mastering this, you not only become a better conversationalist but also someone who can easily handle any social situation. So next time the conversation lulls, remember, it's not a signal to bail —it's your cue to shine.

EXITING CONVERSATIONS SMOOTHLY AND POLITELY

So, you've navigated the tricky waters of kicking off a conversation, danced through the details, and sidestepped a few awkward silences. But all good things—including chitchats—must come to an end. Here's where you get to show off your smooth exit skills because knowing how to gracefully bow out of a conversation is as crucial as learning how to start one. Let's explore how you can leave a conversation without making it look like you're fleeing the scene.

First things first, recognizing natural endpoints in a conversation can be as subtle as catching a yawn or as straightforward as someone glancing at their watch. These are your cues that the curtain is closing on this act of your social play. You might notice the conversation topics are wrapping up or the energy is waning—people might start looking around the room or fiddling with their belongings. These are all your green lights to begin your smooth exit strategy.

Now, on to the actual exciting part. Polite closing remarks are your weapon here.

They're like the cherry on top of your conversational sundae, leaving a sweet taste as you part ways. Phrases like, "I've really enjoyed talking with you" or "It was great catching up, let's do this again soon" keep the tone positive and affirming. These kinds of statements do double duty—signal that you're wrapping up and leave the other person feeling good about the interaction. It's like ending on a high note in a melody; it just feels right.

Making future plans can also be a graceful way to exit. It shows you're interested in continuing the personal or professional relationship. You could say something like, "Let's grab coffee sometime and continue this conversation!" or "I'd love to hear more about your project. Can we touch base next week?" This gives a clear and positive closure to the current conversation and opens the door for future interactions. It's like setting the stage for a sequel to a movie that both of you would want to watch.

Lastly, take into account the power of body language in your exit. How you leave says as much as what you say while leaving. Maintain eye contact to show sincerity as you say your goodbyes. Watch out for going in for a hug as they put out their arm for a handshake; that's just embarrassing. A friendly nod may cement a good impression, depending on how formal the setting is. These physical cues reinforce your words, leaving a lasting positive image of you as you exit the conversation.

Mastering the art of exiting a conversation gracefully ensures the interaction ends on a positive note, making both parties feel respected and valued. It's about closing the loop with the same care and attention you opened it with. By recognizing the right moment to close, using polite and positive phrases, suggesting future engagements, and aligning your body language with your exit intentions, you ensure that your social interactions are as smooth at the end as they were at the start. This way, you leave a lasting, professional, warm impression, setting the stage for continued positive interactions.

WRAPPING UP CHAPTER 2

And there you have it—a complete guide to navigating everyday social interactions like a pro. From breaking the ice confidently to remembering names, diving deeper than small talk, handling the hush of silences, and finally making your exit gracefully, you're now equipped to handle the social seas easily. Each skill builds on the last, turning you into not just a participant but a standout in any social setting.

As we close this chapter, remember that the essence of these interactions isn't just about making a good impression. It's about creating meaningful connections that enrich your life and the lives of others around you. So take these skills, step out confidently, and watch your social landscape transform.

Next, we will dive into building deeper connections. Once you've started the conversation, what comes next is making those interactions count. Stay tuned, and let's keep this conversation going!

CHAPTER 3
BUILDING CONFIDENCE AND OVERCOMING BARRIERS

Ah, confidence—that elusive state of being that seems to waltz effortlessly with some while playing hard to get with others. Think of it as the cool kid at the social skills party. If you've ever felt like you're clinging to the wallflower status, fear not! This chapter is about stepping onto the dance floor of social settings with your head held high. We're not just talking about puffing up your chest and faking it. Nope, we're diving into genuine, rock-solid self-confidence that feels as good as finding extra fries at the bottom of your take-out bag.

STRATEGIES TO BUILD SELF-CONFIDENCE IN SOCIAL SETTINGS

Embrace Vulnerability

Let's kick things off with a real game-changer: vulnerability. Now, before you raise your eyebrows and mumble, "Thanks, but no thanks," hear me out. Vulnerability isn't about wearing your heart on your sleeve so everyone can poke it with a stick. It's about showing up as your genuine self, imperfections and all, and not camping behind a façade. When you open up about your thoughts and feelings, something magical happens—connections deepen, and your confidence gets a turbo boost because being real takes guts. In all of my experiences, being vulnerable and being able to make fun of yourself is a game changer in making connections. People love it, so don't consider it embarrassing; consider it a gateway to friendships.

Take Brené Brown, a researcher and storyteller who champions the power of vulnerability. She argues that vulnerability is the birthplace of love, belonging, joy, and courage. Imagine sharing a personal story at a gathering. Instead of nods of polite approval, you see sparks of genuine interest and nods of "Me too!" That's the sweet spot where barriers break down and honest conversations start. It's like opening the door to let others see the real, unpolished you—and finding out they quite like the view.

Set Achievable Social Goals

Moving on to something a bit more tactical—setting achievable social goals. This isn't about transforming into the life of the party by tomorrow afternoon. It's about small, doable steps that build your social mojo one interaction at a time. Maybe it's saying hi to a neighbor you usually only smile at or asking a co-worker about their weekend plans. These goals should be specific, measurable, and, yeah, a bit of a stretch—but not so daunting that you'd rather binge-watch old sitcoms instead.

Think of it as leveling up in a video game. Each small victory is a confidence coin in your pocket. You start with manageable levels —initiating small talks—and gradually move to boss levels—like mingling at a big social event. And just like in games, every level passed boosts your skills and self-assurance.

Celebrate Small Victories

Speaking of victories, let's remember to celebrate them. And no, you don't need confetti cannons each time you make small talk (though that would be awesome). But acknowledging and rewarding yourself for stepping out of your comfort zone reinforces that you're doing something right. It's like training a puppy with treats. Had a great chat with a stranger at a café? Treat yourself to a victory latte. These celebrations make the journey enjoyable and motivate you to push your boundaries.

Role Models and Mentorship

Last up, let's talk about role models and mentors. These people strut their confidence like they were born with it. Having someone to look up to can guide your path and show you what's possible. It could be a friend who can transform any room they walk into or a public figure whose charisma is off the charts. Reach out, ask for advice, observe what they do and how they interact with others. Most confident people love to share their tips and might even give you direct feedback if you ask nicely. Think of it as getting the cheat codes for social confidence.

Mentors are especially gold when it comes to building confidence. They provide not just inspiration but practical guidance based on their own experiences. They can be your sounding board, your cheerleader, and sometimes, your gentle (or not-so-gentle) push toward more significant challenges. It's like having a personal trainer for your social skills—someone who's invested in seeing you succeed and isn't afraid to make you sweat a bit.

By embracing vulnerability, setting achievable goals, celebrating your wins, and learning from those who've mastered the art, you're building confidence and setting the stage for a richer, more connected social life. So, let's put these strategies into play and watch as doors start opening and conversations flow. Who knows? Maybe you'll be the next social confidence guru someone looks up to! Ready to turn the page and tackle the next set of social skills? Let's do this!

OVERCOMING THE FEAR OF PUBLIC SPEAKING

So, you've been tapped to speak at your best friend's wedding, or your boss thinks you're just the person to present the quarterly report. Great, right? If only your stomach didn't churn like you'd swallowed a live octopus. Fear not! Overcoming the dread of public speaking is like learning to ride a bike—wobbly at first but smooth sailing with some practice. Let's break it down into manageable chunks, starting with the backbone of any good speech: preparation and practice.

Think of your speech or presentation as a road trip. Before you hit the gas, you need a map (your organized content), a clean windshield (rehearsing), and maybe a GPS (cue cards). Start by structuring your content with a clear beginning, middle, and end. Hook your audience early with something intriguing—be it a startling statistic, a joke, or a compelling story. Your roadmap shows where you're heading, making it easier for your audience to follow. Now, about that windshield—rehearsing isn't just about muttering to yourself in the shower. It's about doing dry runs as close to the actual environment as possible. Practicing in front of friends or even your pet goldfish can help you adjust your tone, pace, and gestures. I personally gather around my wife and moaning kids and their friends to listen to my speech. It's family, but getting used to being in front of people is still helpful, and they give you honest feedback about how you presented. Cue cards? They're your presentation's GPS—helpful, but don't stare at them so much that you trip over the scenic views. Keep them brief, with bullet points to jog your memory, and you'll stay on track without reading off them like a robot.

Now, let's talk about those pesky physical symptoms of anxiety— sweaty palms, racing heart, the works. Breathing exercises are your best friend here. Try the 4-7-8 technique: breathe in for four seconds, hold for seven, and exhale for eight. It's like hitting the pause button on your nervous system, telling your body, "Hey, we're cool, no lions here." And right before you go on stage? A few minutes of deep breathing can be as calming as imagining the audience in their underwear (classic advice, but questionable effectiveness). Simple relaxation methods, like progressive muscle relaxation, can also loosen up the tension that makes you feel like a walking ironing board.

Engaging your audience is the secret to distract you from your nerves and make your speech memorable. Ever sat through a presentation that felt as long as a polar night? You want to be something other than that presenter. Keep your audience awake by inviting them into your talk. Ask questions like, "By a show of hands, how many of you have …" or "Can anyone tell me …?" This turns your monologue into a dialogue, making your audience feel involved and keeping their attention locked. Not only that, but I also find getting the audience to participate makes the speech feel less like all eyes are on you and more like a conversation with people, which is a lot less scary. Humor is another golden key. A well-timed joke can lighten the mood and make your audience warm up to you. Just keep it appropriate and relevant—no dad jokes unless you're sure they'll land well. If in doubt, avoid "Why did the chicken cross the road?" territory.

Lastly, the power of visualization shouldn't be underestimated. This isn't about daydreaming that you're on a beach instead of presenting. It's a focused technique where you vividly imagine yourself giving a successful talk. Picture everything—walking confidently onto the stage, the audience's smiling faces, delivering your lines flawlessly, and the hearty applause at the end. Sports psychologists swear by this method to enhance athletic performance, which works just as well for public speaking. Visualizing success programs your brain to follow that path because you've mentally rehearsed it, making it feel familiar and achievable.

By breaking down the process into preparation, relaxation, engagement, and visualization, speaking in public transforms from a sweaty nightmare into another skill you rock. With these tools, you'll deliver your speech effectively and might even enjoy the spotlight. So, please take a deep breath, picture your success, and show them what you've got!

DEALING WITH REJECTION IN SOCIAL CONTEXTS

Oh, rejection. That not-so-sweet sting we've all felt when our well-crafted text is met with a ghostly silence or when we muster every ounce of courage to invite someone out, only to get a "thanks, but no thanks." It's like a punch to the gut, isn't it? But here's the scoop: Rejection is as common as the cold, and it's not the bogeyman we often make it out to be. Let's unravel this tangled web of feelings and find ways to turn rejection from a feared enemy into an unexpected ally.

First off, understanding rejection in its full emotional glory is vital. It hurts because it hits at our basic need to belong, something etched into our DNA. Back in the day, being part of the tribe was crucial for survival, so rejection was literally a life-or-death matter. Fast forward to today, and while being turned down for a date or a job won't jeopardize your survival, that old primal alarm system in your brain doesn't know this. It goes off full blast, making you feel like you're in mortal peril. That's why rejection can feel so significant—so personal. But here's the twist—it's not. It's a normal part of human interactions, as every day as a cup of coffee.

So, how do you reframe this dreaded experience? Start by viewing rejection as a redirection, a nudge toward something or someone better suited for you. It's not a stop sign; it's a detour to a road less traveled but potentially more rewarding. For instance, didn't get the job? Maybe it wasn't the right fit, and there's a position out there that aligns perfectly with your skills. That date said no? Perhaps it frees you to meet someone who really gets your quirky humor. This mindset shift can transform the sting of rejection into a prompt for exploration and new opportunities. Think of it as nature's way of saying, "I've got a better idea!"

Building emotional resilience is your next line of defense. This isn't about developing a thick skin or an I-don't-care attitude; it's about fostering a core of strength that lets you face rejection without letting it shatter your self-worth. Surround yourself with a supportive network—friends, family, and mentors who have your back. Engaging in selfcare practices plays a huge role, too. Whether it's yoga, reading (two of my favorites), or jamming on your guitar, make time for activities that replenish your energy and bring you joy. Keeping a balanced perspective is crucial. Remember, everyone faces rejection. You're not alone in this. Every "no" is a step closer to a "yes."

Let's get a bit scientific with a dash of exposure therapy. This approach involves gradually and repeatedly facing your fear of rejection in controlled, manageable doses. Start small. Ask a friend for a minor favor they might refuse. Apply for a position you think might be a long shot. Go on a date with no expectations. The goal is to desensitize yourself to the fear of rejection, making it less daunting each time. It's like building muscle; the more you flex it, the stronger it becomes. Over time, what once felt like a terrifying leap into the unknown becomes just another step on your path. Who knew getting used to "no" could be part of your workout routine?

As you navigate the rocky terrains of social interactions, remember that dealing with rejection is part of the journey. By understanding its roots, reframing its impact, building resilience, and gently exposing yourself to it, you transform this feared foe into a catalyst for growth and self-discovery. So next time rejection knocks on your door, welcome it in. Sit it down for a chat. You might discover it's not the monster you feared but a guide leading you toward richer, more fulfilling social experiences. Ready to turn the page and see what's next? Let's keep moving forward.

TRANSFORMING NEGATIVE SELF-TALK IN SOCIAL SCENARIOS

Have you ever found yourself mentally replaying a social slip-up like a bad sitcom rerun? Or predicting a social disaster before you even step out the door? That, my friend, is negative self-talk, the uninvited guest at your mental party. It whispers things like, "I'll never be good at this" or "They probably think I'm weird," turning minor missteps into epic tragedies. But guess what? You can kick this party crasher to the curb.

Let's break down how to spot, stop, and swap these pesky thought patterns for something a whole lot cheerier.

First up, identify these gloomy gremlins. Negative self-talk often falls into a few sneaky categories, like catastrophizing, where you expect the worst possible outcome in any situation. Picture this: You're about to enter a party and immediately think, "I'll say something stupid, and everyone will laugh." Or there's mind-reading, where you assume you know what others are thinking—and it's usually something negative. "They're looking at me because they think my outfit is terrible," when they might be admiring your style or not noticing because they're caught up in their own thoughts. Recognizing these patterns is like turning on a light in a dark room. Suddenly, the monsters aren't so scary.

Now, let's get into the nitty-gritty of challenging those irrational thoughts. This is where you play detective and question the evidence behind your negative self-talk. Ask yourself: "What evidence do I have that everyone will laugh at me?" or "Could there be a different reason someone is looking my way?" This step is about poking holes in your initial assumptions and considering alternative explanations. It's like realizing the shadows on your wall aren't monsters; they're just the result of your cat walking past the nightlight. Turns out, the real monster is Mr. Whiskers' late-night escapades.

Replacing these thoughts is where the real magic happens. Instead of "I'll embarrass myself," try "I'm going to meet someone interesting tonight." This isn't about slapping a happy sticker on your worries; it's about shifting your perspective to a more balanced, positive viewpoint. It's training your brain to be a supportive coach rather than a harsh critic. Each positive replacement is a step toward rewiring your thoughts to be more confidence-boosting and less doom-filled.

Mindfulness and awareness are your secret weapons here. Mindfulness keeps you anchored in the present moment, making it easier to catch and adjust negative thoughts as they happen. Try this: next time you're in a social setting and you feel negative self-talk bubbling up, take a moment to focus on your breath or the sensations in your feet. This pulls you back from the spiral of negative thoughts and gives you a chance to reset. It's like hitting the pause button on a video when you realize you're not actually enjoying the plot.

Creating a positive script can turbo-charge this process. Before you step into your next social event, write down or mentally rehearse positive affirmations about how you want the interaction to go, such as "I am calm and articulate" or "I bring positive energy into the room." Think of it as setting the stage for your mind to follow. This script acts like a roadmap, guiding your thoughts to follow a more positive route rather than veering off down the backroads of *Anxietyville*.

Transforming negative self-talk in social scenarios opens a whole new world of more enjoyable and less stress-filled interactions. It's about taking control of the narrative in your head and making it work for you, not against you. By identifying, challenging, replacing negative thoughts, and grounding yourself with mindfulness, you're not just improving your social skills but also enhancing your overall mental well-being. So next time you catch yourself being a Debbie Downer in your head, remember that you have the tools to turn that frown upside down and give every social encounter a chance to shine.

USING AFFIRMATIONS TO ENHANCE SOCIAL COMPETENCE

Imagine you've got a tiny cheerleader in your pocket, always ready to chant personalized encouragements just for you. That's what affirmations are like—mini pep talks you give yourself to boost confidence and transform your mindset, especially in social settings where nerves might otherwise get the better of you. Crafting these affirmations effectively is both an art and a science. They should be specific, positive, and present tense, focusing on what you want to feel and achieve, not what you wish to avoid.

Let's break it down with an example. Say you're nervous about attending a networking event. Instead of a vague affirmation like "I am good at meeting people," dial it up to "I am confidently introducing myself to new people with ease and enthusiasm tonight." See the difference? The second is not only specific and positive; it's also in the present tense, planting the idea that this is already happening. It's about setting the stage in your mind and giving your brain a script for a blockbuster performance.

Now, how do you weave these affirmations into the fabric of your daily life? It's simpler than you might think. One of the most effective methods is to say them out loud to yourself in front of a mirror. Yes, it might feel a bit awkward at first, talking to your reflection like it's your best friend. But seeing yourself saying these positive words helps reinforce the message—think of it as syncing audio with visuals for a more profound impact. Another great tool is writing them down in a journal. This act of writing serves as a reminder and helps you internalize the affirmations. If you're tech-savvy, setting them as reminders on your smartphone can ping you with these positive notes throughout the day, weaving positivity through your daily routine like a golden thread.

Affirmations can and should be tailored to different social scenarios to maximize effectiveness. For instance, if you're going on a date and feeling jittery, an affirmation like "I am enjoying a fun and relaxed conversation with my date" can set a positive expectation. Or if you're about to tackle a group project, telling yourself, "I am contributing valuable ideas and collaborating well with my team," primes you for proactive engagement. Each scenario demands a slightly different set of affirmations, customized to address specific anxieties and boost the needed social skills, like having a wardrobe full of pep talks for every occasion.

Evaluating the impact of these affirmations is crucial because, let's face it, not every phrase you tell yourself will hit the mark right away. It's about fine-tuning. After using an affirmation, you noted that you felt more relaxed but less engaged than you'd hoped. No problem! Adjust it. Perhaps you need something more direct, like, "I am fully present and actively participating in discussions." The key is to reflect on what felt off and tweak your affirmations to better align with your psychological needs and the social goals you're aiming to achieve.

By integrating these personalized, positive affirmations into your daily routine, you're not just prepping for social success but also building a mindset that embraces and enhances your social competence. Each affirmation is a stepping stone toward a more confident and socially skilled you, transforming how you see yourself and interact with others.

As we wrap up this chapter on building confidence and overcoming barriers, we've armed ourselves with practical strategies ranging from embracing vulnerability and setting achievable goals to mastering the art of affirmations. Each tool and technique builds on the last, creating a robust framework that supports social success and a deeper, more satisfying engagement with the world around us. Moving forward, we delve deeper into the nuances of creating and sustaining relationships because what's a social butterfly without a garden in which to flourish? Let's continue to unfold these skills together, transforming challenges into opportunities for growth.

CHAPTER 4
DIGITAL COMMUNICATION IN THE SOCIAL MEDIA AGE

W elcome to the digital jungle! It's a wild, sometimes wonderful, often wacky world where emojis reign supreme and where "LOL" doesn't always mean someone's actually laughing out loud. In this chapter, we'll navigate the realm of digital communication—think of it as learning to speak all over again, but this time with your thumbs.

CRAFTING ENGAGING TEXT MESSAGES

Conciseness and Clarity

Have you ever received a text message that's so long you need to take a coffee break halfway through reading it? Or one so cryptic that it feels like cracking the Da Vinci code? Neither is ideal. In the realm of texting, the golden rule is to keep it clear and concise. Your goal is to convey your message without giving the reader a headache or a reason to misunderstand your intent.

So, how do you strike this balance? Start by getting straight to the point. If you're meeting someone and running late, a simple "Hey, got caught in traffic. Be there in 15. Sorry!" does the trick. It's straightforward, polite, and informative. Avoid the fluff—texts aren't the place for lengthy pleasantries. Think of each message as a mini billboard; you have limited space to convey your message clearly and impactfully. After all, nobody wants to read a novel-length text when a sentence will do. Save the epic sagas for your memoirs.

Tone and Formality

Texting your buddy and texting your boss is not the same ball game. One might be filled with GIFs and "LOLs," while the other requires more polish. Gauging the appropriate tone and level of formality is crucial in digital communication. You wouldn't send a meme to your boss about being late, right? A simple "Good morning, I'm running a bit behind schedule but should arrive shortly. Thank you for your understanding" keeps it professional and respectful.

Choosing the wrong tone can lead to messages that either come off as too stiff or overly casual, which might confuse or alienate the recipient. When in doubt, err on being slightly more formal. Use cues from how the other person communicates to adjust your tone accordingly. Think of it this way: You wouldn't wear flip-flops to a black-tie event, so don't send emojis to a formal request (unless you're sure your boss loves a good smiley face).

Use of Emojis and Multimedia

Emojis, GIFs, and memes can be the salt and pepper of texting—they enhance the flavor, but too much can ruin the dish. These colorful characters and images can help convey tone and emotion, often lost in plain text. A smiley face at the end of a message can soften a request, making it friendlier, while a well-timed GIF can break the tension in a conversation and bring about a laugh.

However, the key is moderation and context. Overusing emojis or picking ones that can be misinterpreted might confuse the message or appear unprofessional. It's also wise to consider the recipient—while your best friend might appreciate a barrage of heart emojis, your new co-worker might not.

Timing and Frequency

Timing is everything. Bombarding someone with texts can feel overwhelming, while taking days to respond can come off as disinterested or rude. The trick is finding a rhythm that works for you and your texting partner. Pay attention to how quickly they respond and try to match their pace. If it's a professional exchange, responding within a few hours during business hours shows promptness and respect for the recipient's time.

Also, consider time zones, especially when texting someone from a different part of the world. A text sent during your lunchtime might jolt someone awake at 3 a.m. on the other side of the globe. A helpful tip is to acknowledge the time difference with a message like, "Good morning from this side of the world! I hope you're having a great day." It shows consideration and keeps you from being that person who texts at unholy hours. Remember, just because you're a night owl doesn't mean everyone else wants to hoot along with you.

By mastering the art of crafting engaging text messages, you can improve your personal and professional relationships and avoid potential digital faux pas. Remember, every text you send is a reflection of you, so let's make each one count! Ready to tackle the next digital communication challenge? Keep those thumbs ready; there's more to learn!

Social Media Dos and Don'ts

Navigating the bustling superhighways of social media can sometimes feel like trying to stick to a diet in a candy store—overwhelming and fraught with temptations. But fear not! With a few smart strategies up your sleeve, you can manage your social media presence like a pro, ensuring it reflects your best self, whether connecting with friends or curating a professional persona. Let's dive into crafting a stellar social media profile, sharing content wisely, engaging gracefully, and sidestepping potential pitfalls.

Profile Management

Think of your social media profile as your digital front porch. It's what people see first, and we all know first impressions matter. Start with your profile picture. There are better places for that blurry photo where you're vaguely recognizable. Choose a clear, friendly, and appropriate picture that says, "Hey, nice to meet you!" For personal accounts, a warm, inviting image does wonders. Consider a headshot for professional accounts where you look approachable and ready to get down to business. Next up, your bio. This little blurb can pack a punch. It's your mini advertisement to the world. Keep it concise but expressive. Share a bit about what makes you tick, your interests, or what you do. Just remember, this is a public space, so keep things you wouldn't shout in a crowded room out of your bio. No need to share that you once ate a whole pizza by yourself. I only did that once in college, so I get a pass.

Adjusting your privacy settings is like setting the rules for who gets past your digital velvet rope. Take control over who sees what. Keeping some photos or posts just for friends and family is okay. Most platforms offer a range of settings that let you customize who can view your posts, tag you, or even comment on your content. Spend some time exploring these options. A well-managed profile is a reflection of you and a fortress that keeps digital chaos at bay.

Content Sharing

Sharing content on social media is an art form. What you share paints a picture of who you are. Think about the palette you choose. Is it colorful, professional, humorous, or educational? Whatever your style, ensure it's consistent and accurate to who you are. But here's the kicker—always think about the long-term impact of what you're posting. That rant about your boss or that wild party photo might seem fun now, but it's not just your friends peeping at your posts. Future employers, your grandma, or your next date might be scrolling through your history. Stick to content you'd be comfortable with anyone seeing, even years later. Remember, the internet never forgets, even if you do.

When it comes to different platforms, tailor your content to fit the culture of each. Instagram loves visuals so that stunning sunset photo goes here. LinkedIn is your professional mega-phone, perfect for sharing the article you wrote on market trends.

Twitter? It's all about snappy, engaging comments on breaking news or hot topics.

Matching your content to the platform not only boosts your posts' effectiveness but also shows you're savvy about the nuances of digital communication. It's like wearing the right outfit for the occasion—you wouldn't show up at a wedding in a tracksuit, right?

Interacting with Others

The comment sections and DMs are where the magic—and the mayhem—happen.

Engaging with others on social media should be like attending a lively dinner party. Be polite, be respectful, and be engaging. When you comment on someone's post, add something meaningful to the conversation. A simple "Great post!" is fine, but a "Great post! Your point about X really made me think about Y..." is better. It shows you're not just passing by—you're engaging thoughtfully.

Handling disagreements publicly can be tricky. Don't type it out if you wouldn't say it in front of a crowded room. Keep your cool. If things get heated, take the high road. Offer a polite rebuttal or agree to disagree, and if necessary, continue the discussion privately. This helps maintain your dignity and reputation, showing you can handle hot topics without getting burned. I like to equate online spats with quicksand—the more you struggle, the deeper you sink.

Avoiding Common Pitfalls

Now, for the potholes to avoid: Oversharing is at the top of the list of don'ts. Before you post, ask yourself, "Is this necessary? Is it relevant?" Keep your private life just that— private. Avoid airing dirty laundry or sharing personal grievances. It's not just about privacy; it's about creating a positive digital footprint you're proud to show off.

Another must is steering clear of controversial topics without tact. Sure, speak your mind on issues you care about, but do it with respect and consideration for differing viewpoints. Ignoring cultural and contextual nuances can also lead your well-intentioned posts astray. Always be aware of the broader context of your audience. What's funny in one culture can be a faux pas in another. Do your homework before you post, especially if your friend list is as diverse as the United Nations.

Navigating social media smartly means managing your profile, sharing content thoughtfully, interacting gracefully, and sidestepping the traps that can snare the unwary. With these strategies, you're not just avoiding pitfalls but also setting yourself up for a richer, more positive social media experience. So post that carefully chosen profile pic, share that insightful article, and comment confidently. Your digital world awaits, and now you're ready to make it your own.

MAINTAINING AUTHENTICITY ONLINE

In the digital age, where your next tweet could go viral or your latest Instagram post might define you, keeping it real is more than just a catchy hashtag; it's a necessity. Let's talk about why it's crucial to have your online self-mirror your offline self and how to maintain authenticity across your digital interactions. Think of your online persona as your personal brand. Like in real life, you want this brand to reflect your true personality, values, and beliefs. It's tempting to create an "ideal" version of yourself online, but let's face it—keeping up with that can be as exhausting as running a marathon in flip-flops. Plus, people connect with authenticity. They want to interact with real humans, not curated avatars.

The key here is consistency. Your online interactions should align with how you behave in the real world. If you're known for your wicked sense of humor offline, let that shine through in your tweets and posts. If you're a thoughtful listener at work, carry that into how you respond to comments on LinkedIn. This consistency reinforces who you are and builds trust with your audience. They know that the person behind the screen is genuine and that what they see is what they get. But here's where it gets tricky— transparency.

Being transparent means being open about your thoughts and feelings and knowing where to draw the line. Yes, share your successes and even some struggles (because everyone loves a comeback story), but remember that the internet never forgets. Before you post, ask yourself if this is something you'd be comfortable with everyone knowing— your boss, your grandma, or even a future employer. It's about finding the sweet spot between being open and maintaining a bit of mystery.

Now, on to building genuine relationships online. This digital world offers incredible tools for staying connected, but the challenge is to make these connections meaningful. It's not just about racking up followers or getting likes; it's about engaging in honest conversations. Show genuine interest in what others say, respond to comments with thoughtful replies, and share content that adds value, not just noise. Think about creating a dialogue, not a monologue. And remember, consistency is key. Regularly interacting with your network keeps the relationship alive and kicking.

When it comes to professional settings, the line between personal and professional can sometimes blur, especially online. Platforms like LinkedIn are great for showcasing your professional achievements, but they also benefit from a touch of individual flair. Share articles related to your field, but don't be afraid to post about a team-building event or a work-related challenge you overcame. This shows that you're not just a resume but a relatable person. Balancing professionalism with a personal touch can enhance your credibility and make you more approachable.

By focusing on these aspects of digital communication, you're not just building a profile; you're building a reputation. Whether through concise and clear text messages, thoughtful social media interactions, or professional online engagements, the digital you should be an authentic reflection of the real you. So, next time you log in, remember that authenticity is your best online strategy. Keep it real, keep it you, and watch your digital relationships flourish as robustly as those in the real world. After all, the world could use a lot more real and a lot less filter.

MANAGING MISUNDERSTANDINGS IN DIGITAL CONVERSATIONS

Navigating the digital conversation highway can sometimes feel like trying to direct traffic in Times Square on New Year's Eve—chaotic, loud, and ripe for misunderstandings. Whether it's a misread text, an email that didn't land as intended, or a social media post that started a war in the comments, digital miscommunications are as common as cat videos on the internet. But fear not; there are ways to clear up the digital fog and reduce the chances of these misunderstandings escalating into digital drama.

Clarification Techniques

The first step in avoiding misunderstandings is ensuring you're on the same page from the start. This means getting your digital detective hat on, being bold, and asking for clarification. But here's the kicker: it's not just about what you ask, but how you ask it. Phrasing is everything. Instead of appearing accusatory, think,

"Why would you say that?" and opt for open-ended questions that invite explanation without putting the other person on the defensive. Try, "Can you help me understand what you meant by that?" It's like offering a handshake instead of a fist. If you have ever been inside the social media comments section, you'll mostly see a lot of fists. Be different. Be the handshake.

Paraphrasing is another nifty tool in your clarification toolkit. It's about repeating what was said in your own words. Think of it as offering a mirror to the speaker, showing them what their message looked like from your side of the screen. "So, just to make sure I'm getting this right, you're saying ..." This shows that you're actively engaged and gives them a chance to correct any misinterpretations before they become bigger issues. It's like checking your rearview mirror before you change lanes—just a quick check to ensure everything's clear.

Apology and Correction

Now, let's say the misunderstanding has already happened. Maybe you misread a message, or perhaps autocorrect turned your innocent text into something bizarre or offensive. This is where the art of the digital apology comes into play. Here's the thing about apologies—they need to be as sincere online as they are in person. A simple, timely "I'm sorry for the confusion, I meant to say this ..." can go a long way in smoothing over digital ruffles.

Correcting misinformation is just as crucial. If you've spread something that turns out wrong, own up to it swiftly. Update your post, send a follow-up text or email explaining the mistake, and provide the correct information. Think of it as hitting the undo button; it might not erase the mistake entirely, but it shows you're committed to setting the record straight.

Preventive Measures

As the old saying goes, an ounce of prevention is worth a pound of cure. This is especially true in digital communication, where deleting a sent message isn't always an option. Start with proof-reading. A quick double-check of your texts or emails can catch those potentially embarrassing typos or autocorrect disasters before they go out. It's the digital equivalent of checking your zipper before you leave the house. This small step can prevent considerable embarrassment.

Cultural differences can also be a landmine in digital communica-tion. Words and phrases that are harmless in one culture can be volatile in another. So, if you're messaging someone from a different background, a quick Google search to understand their cultural context can prevent a lot of misunderstandings. Lastly, steer clear of ambiguous language. Be as clear and direct as possi-ble. It's like giving someone directions; the more straightforward it is, the less chance they have of ending up lost.

Handling Escalated Situations

Despite your best efforts, sometimes things escalate. Knowing how to de-escalate when a digital conversation starts heading south can keep a minor misunderstanding from turning into a full-blown conflict. One effective strategy is to take the conversation offline. A phone call or a face-to-face meeting can resolve issues more effectively than a text or email chain. My wife and I use this all the time. Suppose something comes across where one of us needs clarification of the intent. In that case, we always call each other rather than try to straighten it out over text and have it snowball. Talking on the phone enables us to get the exact message across with the correct intent. It's easier to convey tone and intent and less likely to leave room for further misunderstandings.

When tensions are high and an offline conversation isn't possible, sometimes bringing in a third party can help mediate. Just make sure it's someone both parties trust to be impartial. It's like having a referee in a sports game—sometimes, you need someone to help call the shots fairly to prevent a total knockout.

By mastering these strategies—from asking the right questions to offering sincere apologies, taking preventive steps, and knowing when to take things offline—you can navigate the digital world with fewer misunderstandings and more meaningful interactions. Remember, every text, email, and post can build bridges or burn them. Choose your words wisely, and let's make every digital interaction count!

THE ETIQUETTE OF DIGITAL DISAGREEMENTS

Ah, the digital age, where disagreements are as common as cat memes on your feed. It's easy to find yourself in a heated debate about pineapple on pizza (we all know the correct answer to this one, right?) or more serious topics like politics. But here's the thing: Not every online spat has to end in virtual fisticuffs or a block-fest. Unless, of course, someone chooses pineapple on their pizza. Just kidding ... or am I? Anyway, there's an art to disagreeing without turning your digital space into a battleground, starting with respect.

When expressing differing opinions online, think of it as a sophisticated dance rather than a mud-slinging contest. Use diplomatic language that keeps the door open for discussion rather than slamming it shut. For instance, phrases like "I see your point, but I feel differently because ..." allow you to present your perspective without discounting the other person's view. This acknowledges their viewpoint, which can keep the tone civil and the conversation constructive. It's about crafting your words to respect the person behind the screen, remembering there's a human on the other side, not just pixels and text.

Now, let's move on to choosing your battles because, let's face it, not every disagreement deserves your two cents. Before diving into the digital fray, take a breath and ask yourself if this is worth your time and energy. Is the issue significant? Can the discussion be productive? Suppose it's just a matter of differing tastes or minor preferences. In that case, it might be wiser to scroll on and save your energy for debates where you can truly make an impact or where the outcome is meaningful. Remember, just because you can have an opinion on everything doesn't mean you should.

But here's the kicker: the impact on your relationships. Oh, it can be lasting! A spur-of the-moment snarky comment can bruise friendships or professional connections, sometimes beyond repair. Digital words are like tattoos; they can be permanent, searchable, and highly visible. Always consider the potential long-term effects of a heated debate on your relationships. It might be time to step back if the risk outweighs the reward. Preserve those bridges rather than burn them over something fleeting. It's about playing the long game in maintaining healthy, respectful online and offline relationships.

Exiting a heated discussion online with grace is almost an art form. When you sense a conversation is going nowhere or the heat levels are rising past comfort, it's wise to bow out politely. A simple "I think we'll have to agree to disagree on this one. Thanks for sharing your thoughts!" can be your exit cue. It shows you're bowing out respectfully without conceding your stance or undermining theirs. This approach keeps your digital dignity intact and leaves the door open for future, more positive interactions.

Navigating the choppy waters of online disagreements with tact and respect isn't just about preserving peace or avoiding conflict. It's an essential component of building and maintaining a mature online presence. It reflects your ability to handle complex interactions and shows you value relationships over winning an argument. So, the next time you find yourself in a digital disagreement, take a moment to choose your words wisely, consider the stakes, and, if needed, make a graceful exit. Your digital self will thank you!

WRAPPING UP DIGITAL COMMUNICATION

Navigating the digital world with savvy and etiquette isn't just a skill; it's necessary in our interconnected age. Every interaction you have shapes your digital footprint, from crafting concise text messages and managing your social media presence to maintaining authenticity and handling disagreements gracefully. It's about more than just keeping up appearances; it's about building genuine connections, fostering positive interactions, and creating a space that reflects your best version.

As we close this chapter on digital communication, remember that each swipe, like, comment, or share is a reflection of you. Use these tools wisely to enhance your relationships and build bridges, not barriers. Next, we dive into the world of creating deeper connections, exploring how these digital skills translate into lasting, meaningful relationships. Stay tuned, and let's keep the conversation going!

CHAPTER 5
ADVANCED COMMUNICATION SKILLS

E ver felt like you're just winging it when you try to get your point across? Whether you're convincing your friends to try that new taco place or pitching your latest big idea at work, knowing how to persuade effectively can feel empowering. I'm going to show you just how easy it can be; you just need to master a few key principles. Welcome to the dojo of persuasion, where your words can move mountains or at least convince someone to move off the couch.

PERSUASION TECHNIQUES FOR POSITIVE INFLUENCE

Understanding the Principles of Persuasion

Let's start with the basics. Persuasion isn't about manipulation or arm-twisting; it's an art form based on psychological principles that can help you influence others ethically. These principles include reciprocity, scarcity, authority, consistency, liking, and consensus.

Reciprocity is like the boomerang of the social psychology world: give something (like a compliment, a small favor, or a piece of gum), and you're likely to get something back. Scarcity, conversely, makes anything seem more desirable simply because it seems less available. Does "limited-time offer" sound familiar? My wife falls for this one all too often in her shopping sprees. One "last chance" sale and our house is suddenly a warehouse.

Authority is all about credibility. People tend to listen to experts, so showing you know your stuff can go a long way. Consistency is when you gently nudge someone to agree with you by getting them to commit to an idea that aligns with their previous behaviors or statements. It's like saying, "Since you loved the first book in the series, you'll probably love the sequel too!" You should hear that one from me in the future. So keep an eye out. Shameless plug, I know.

Liking—well, it's hard to resist someone you like. If people feel connected to you, they're more likely to be swayed by your words. Lastly, there's consensus, which plays on the idea that we look to others to determine our own actions: "Nine out of ten people recommend ..." is persuasive because it confirms a group consensus. Which is why you should leave a review of this book for me on Amazon. Okay, I'll stop.

Building Credibility

Now, let's talk about building your credibility. It's tough to persuade anyone if they don't trust you or believe in your expertise. Start by backing up your claims with facts, statistics, or sources. It's like bringing a well-documented blueprint to a team meeting; it shows you've done your homework.

But here's the kicker: credibility isn't just about what you know; it's also about how you convey it. Be confident but not cocky. Speak clearly and assertively but keep your tone friendly and approachable. Think of it as the cool teacher everyone respected in school— the one who could make even calculus seem cool because they were passionate and knew their stuff inside out. Well, maybe not calculus, but you get my point.

Emotional Appeals

Moving on to emotional appeals, let's face it: we're all a little ruled by our hearts. Crafting messages that resonate emotionally can significantly boost your persuasive power. Storytelling is a fantastic tool here. A well-told story can transport listeners, stir emotions, and drive home your point more effectively than a dry recitation of facts. Use vivid language to paint pictures in the mind's eye. It's not just a used car; it's "a trusted companion that's been part of many family adventures, reliable, and ready for many more."

Balancing Logic and Emotion

Finally, balancing logic and emotion in your persuasion efforts is like being a DJ mixing tracks. Lean too hard on emotion, and you risk seeming manipulative or sappy; overdo the logic, and you could come off as cold or robotic. The key is to weave facts and feelings together so seamlessly that your audience is intellectually and emotionally moved. Present logical arguments, then amplify them with emotional undertones that resonate with your audience's values and experiences.

Imagine discussing the idea of moving to a new city or even a new part of town with your partner. If you lean too heavily on emotional reasons, like "I just feel like this place isn't for us anymore," it might sound impulsive or vague. On the other hand, if you focus solely on logical reasons, such as "The job market in the new city offers a 10 percent higher average salary," it might seem like you're ignoring the emotional aspect of such a big decision.

A balanced approach would be to combine these elements: "I've been thinking about how we can grow and find new opportunities, and the job market in the new city offers a 10 percent higher average salary. But, more importantly, I think the change of scenery and the cultural experiences there could bring us closer and give us a fresh start. It feels like a place where we could both professionally and personally thrive." Aren't you ready to move after hearing that?

In the workplace, if you're trying to persuade your team to adopt a new project management tool, start with the logical benefits (e.g., "It's proven to reduce project completion times by 30 percent"). Then, layer on the emotional appeal by highlighting how much smoother their day-to-day operations will be with less stress about deadlines and more time for creative tasks.

By mastering these techniques—understanding the principles of persuasion, building credibility, making emotional appeals, and balancing logic with emotion—you'll be well-equipped to influence others personally and professionally. Whether you're aiming to sway your boss or win over a new client, these skills will ensure your arguments are heard, felt, and acted upon. Now, let's keep this momentum going as we dive deeper into the nuances of effective communication.

NEGOTIATION SKILLS FOR EVERYDAY SITUATIONS

Imagine you're at a flea market. You've set your eyes on this vintage lamp, and you're about to enter the delicate dance of negotiation. Or maybe you're not haggling over decor but trying to convince your roommate to stop leaving dishes in the sink. Whether you're bargaining in a bazaar or reaching a peaceful household agreement, negotiation skills are your secret handshake into the world of getting what you want without turning it into a Wild West showdown.

Preparation and Goal Setting

First things first: preparation is your best friend in any negotiation. It's like going on a road trip; you wouldn't just jump in the car without knowing your destination and the route, right? Unless you're a nomad at heart, those people are cool. But let's say you're more like me. Start by understanding your own goals clearly. What exactly do you want to achieve from this negotiation? Are you looking for a raise, a better deal on your car insurance, or just for your roommate to agree to a cleaning schedule? Knowing this sets the framework for your negotiation strategy.

Next up, put yourself in the shoes of the other party. What might they want?

Understanding their goals isn't just about empathy; it's strategic. It helps you anticipate their moves and prepare counteroffers. If your roommate hates vacuuming but doesn't mind doing dishes, you've got a chip to play. Finally, think about the possible outcomes.

What's your best-case scenario? What's your walk-away point? Setting these boundaries for yourself helps keep the negotiation from veering off into emotional territory and keeps things professional and productive.

Effective Communication Techniques in Negotiation

Now, let's discuss how to communicate during a negotiation. It's not just about what you say but also how you say it. Active listening is crucial. This means really hearing what the other person is saying and showing them you understand. Nodding, maintaining eye contact, and repeating what you've heard (without turning it into a parrot show) are all part of this dance. It shows respect and builds trust, and people are more likely to cooperate if they feel respected.

Clear articulation of your needs and wants is equally essential. Be direct and transparent about what you're looking for. Muddying the waters with vague statements or hidden agendas can backfire, making the negotiation more complicated and less likely to succeed. And remember the power of strategic questioning. Asking the right questions gives you more information. It can guide the negotiation in the direction you want it to go. Open-ended questions that start with "what" or "how" can encourage the other party to reveal more of their position and potentially open new pathways to agreement.

Bargaining Strategies

Choosing the right bargaining strategy can make or break a negotiation. There are generally two types: competitive and collaborative. Competitive bargaining is what you see in movies: hardball, high stakes, and often a winner-takes-all attitude. It's helpful when you don't need to worry about the relationship with the other person and you're not likely to see them again—like that flea market lamp.

Collaborative bargaining, on the other hand, is about finding a win-win solution. It's the strategy to go for when you want to preserve the relationship, and both parties need to feel good about the outcome. This could be negotiating with a business partner, a coworker, or, yes, that roommate situation. It involves more communication, empathy, and, often, creativity in finding solutions that satisfy everyone.

Closing and Agreement

Finally, effectively closing a negotiation is about ensuring clarity and satisfaction for all parties involved. Once you've hammered out the details, summarize the agreement to make sure everyone is on the same page. This recap can prevent future misunderstandings and show that you're committed to a transparent and honest negotiation process.

If the negotiation is formal, like a job contract or a large business deal, make sure everything is put in writing. This isn't just about formality; it's about having a straightforward document that outlines the agreement, which can be invaluable if questions or disputes arise later. A well-drafted contract can save you from heaps of headaches down the road.

By honing these negotiation skills—from preparation to effective communication, choosing the right strategy, and closing the deal— you equip yourself with the tools to navigate the major negotiations of your life and the everyday little talks that shape your world. So the next time you find yourself in a negotiation, big or small, remember these steps and play your cards right. Who knows? You might walk away with more than you hoped for.

ADVANCED EMPATHY: CONNECTING ON A DEEPER LEVEL

Ever met someone who just gets you? Not just on the surface level but really understand the gears turning in your head? That's advanced empathy in action—like empathy with a PhD. While basic empathy lets us recognize and feel for others' emotions, advanced empathy digs deeper, giving us a near-psychic ability to grasp the unspoken thoughts and feelings behind those emotions. It's like being an emotional archaeologist, gently brushing away the surface to reveal the hidden layers.

So, how do you develop this superpower? It starts with empathetic listening, which goes beyond nodding and making the right noises at the correct times. This type of listening is about fully immersing yourself in the other person's emotional world. Picture it like diving into a novel; you're not just skimming the pages but living inside the story, feeling what the characters feel. In real-world terms, it means paying attention not just to the words being said but to the tone, the pauses, and the sighs—everything that adds color and depth to the spoken narrative.

When you engage in this kind of listening, respond in ways that validate and explore these deeper feelings. It's not about offering a quick fix or advice unless specifically requested. Instead, try echoing their feelings back to them with phrases like, "It sounds like you're really passionate about this" or "That must have been really challenging for you." This doesn't just show that you're listening; it shows you're connecting on a deeper emotional level. It's about giving them space to explore their feelings further, which can be incredibly affirming and healing. You're saying, "I get you," in the most heartfelt way possible.

Handling emotional disclosures is another crucial aspect. When someone trusts you enough to share their deep vulnerabilities, they're handing you a piece of their heart. The way you handle this can strengthen or weaken your bond. The key is to maintain composure, provide support, and use empathy to de-escalate potential conflicts that might arise from these intense exchanges. For instance, if a friend is upset and their words become heated, acknowledging their feelings can help soothe the immediacy of their emotions. Say something like, "I can see this is really upsetting you, and that's completely understandable." This empathetic response can help cool down a heated moment, paving the way for a calmer, more constructive dialogue.

Applying Empathy in Diverse Settings

But here's where it gets fascinating—applying empathy in diverse cultural and social settings. Our world is full of vibrant and varied cultures, each with its own values, norms, and emotional expressions. What's considered a typical display of emotion in one culture might be seen as overly subdued or excessively dramatic in another. Advanced empathy involves sensitivity to these differences and adjusting your emotional responses accordingly.

For example, in some cultures, direct eye contact is seen as a sign of respect and honesty; in others, it might be perceived as aggressive. Being aware of these nuances can help you navigate cross-cultural interactions more smoothly. Say you're working with a team from multiple cultural backgrounds. Showing that you respect and understand each person's cultural context can make everyone feel more valued and understood, fostering a more inclusive and harmonious work, school, or even extended family environment.

By embracing and practicing advanced empathy, you enhance your personal relationships and boost your professional interactions. It's a skill that echoes across all aspects of life, enriching your connections and deepening your understanding of the human experience. So next time you find yourself in a conversation, try tapping into that deep well of empathy. Listen not just with your ears but with your heart. It may change what you see and, more importantly, how you respond.

THE POWER OF STORYTELLING IN PERSONAL CONNECTIONS

Imagine sitting around a campfire, the flames casting playful shadows as someone begins to weave a tale. The crackling fire fades into the background as the story takes center stage, drawing everyone into a shared experience. This scene captures the essence of storytelling, an age-old art that remains one of the most powerful ways to connect personally and professionally with others.

Let's dissect the anatomy of compelling storytelling. First, there's the structure—every compelling story has a clear beginning, middle, and end. The spine holds the narrative together, guiding the listener through the journey without losing them along the way. The beginning sets the scene and hooks the listener; the middle builds tension or challenges; and the end resolves the conflict, providing closure or a punchline that leaves the listener satisfied or perhaps wanting more.

Then, there are the characters—the heartbeats of your story. Compelling characters are relatable; they reflect real emotions and dilemmas. They don't have to be heroes or villains; they just need to be authentic, allowing the listener to see parts of themselves in the story. Conflict, the narrative's engine, introduces the characters' challenges or obstacles. It engages the story, pushing the narrative forward and keeping the listener invested. Imagine a story without conflict, a soap opera without drama—utterly pointless.

Finally, the resolution is where the conflict finds its peace, offering new insights or changes in the characters and ideally leaving your audience with something to ponder or cherish.

Transitioning from the elements to application, personal stories are like bridges built of words that connect us to others. Sharing personal experiences isn't just about recounting events but about conveying values, emotions, and insights in a way that resonates. When you share how you felt during your first public speaking event or recount the mixed feelings of leaving home for college, you're offering more than a story; you're extending a handout, inviting others to connect with you on a human level. This doesn't just build rapport; it fosters trust and understanding, laying down the roots for deeper relationships. Remember, anything other than talking about the weather.

In professional settings, storytelling transforms from a personal connection tool into a strategic communication technique. Imagine you're leading a meeting or giving a presentation. You make your content informative and memorable by embedding facts and data within a narrative about real-world impacts or a case study that highlights challenges and solutions. Stories can encapsulate complex information in a digestible format, making it easier for your audience to understand, remember, and feel motivated by what you're saying. Whether inspiring your team with a story of a past project that turned around against all odds or persuading stakeholders with a narrative that aligns your proposal with the company's vision, storytelling in business is about moving people to action by engaging their minds and emotions.

Practicing Storytelling

Now, how do you become a master storyteller? Practice, of course, but let's make it fun. Start with exercises that sharpen your skills. One effective method is to take a mundane event and make it enjoyable. Consider recounting your morning routine but frame it as an epic adventure. "This morning, I embarked on a perilous journey to conquer the kingdom of Caffeina, battling the treacherous Traffic Titan and the Tempest of Lost Keys." It sounds silly, but it's a playful way to practice giving life to ordinary events. Plus, you'll never look at your commute the same way again. Thank me later.

Another exercise is to craft stories from your life experiences. Use the structure of the beginning, middle, and end to outline your narrative. Focus on portraying characters authentically and building an engaging and relatable conflict. Share these stories with friends or family and ask for feedback. What resonated? What felt flat? This feedback is gold—it's like having a test audience for your personal screenplay.

Lastly, consider the delivery of your stories. How you tell a story can be as important as the story itself. Practice varying your tone, pace, and volume to match the emotional arc of the narrative. Use pauses to build suspense or emphasize points. Remember, storytelling is a performance, and you are the director, actor, and narrator all in one. Whether you aim to inspire, educate, or entertain, your ability to tell a compelling story can be the key to unlocking deeper connections, driving motivation, and bringing ideas to life. So gather your audience at the campfire or the conference room and spin a tale that leaves them enchanted and enlightened.

MASTERING THE ART OF GIVING AND RECEIVING FEEDBACK

Let's face it: feedback is like a double-edged sword—it can sting but sharpen. Whether you're on the giving or receiving end, handling feedback is an art form that can elevate your personal and professional relationships to new heights. So, buckle up! We're about to take a deep dive into transforming feedback from a dreaded encounter into a powerful tool for growth. Grab your helmets, folks, because this ride will be bumpy and enlightening.

Principles of Constructive Feedback

Constructive feedback is all about building up, not tearing down. It's like being a coach rather than a critic. The first principle here is specificity. Vague comments like "You need to do better" are about as helpful as a chocolate teapot. Instead, pinpoint exactly what needs improvement and why. For instance, saying, "I noticed you struggled to keep the meeting on track today. Perhaps next time, a structured agenda might help keep everything flowing smoothly," provides a clear, actionable suggestion.

Timeliness is another crucial factor. Feedback is most effective when given in the heat of the moment—or at least while the details are fresh. Waiting six months to tell someone their presentation skills needed work back in January? Not so helpful. It's about striking while the iron is hot, so the feedback can be immediately applied and the lessons swiftly integrated.

Finally, always focus on behavior, not personality. Feedback should never feel like a personal attack. It's not about changing who someone is; it's about improving how they do things. So instead of saying, "You're disorganized," try, "I've noticed that organizing your workspace could help streamline your workflow."

This shifts the focus from what they are to what they can do differently, which is much easier to digest and act upon.

Receiving Feedback Gracefully

On the flip side, receiving feedback can sometimes feel like swallowing a bitter pill. The key is to listen actively, keep an open mind, and resist the urge to get defensive. This doesn't mean you have to agree with everything that's said, but rather that you're willing to hear it out and consider its validity. Think of it as mining for gold—you might have to sift through some dirt to find the nuggets of truth that will help you grow.

Asking clarifying questions can also help you get the most out of feedback. If something needs to be clarified, ask for specific examples. For instance, if someone tells you that you need to improve your communication skills, you might respond with, "Could you give me an example of a time when my communication fell short?" This helps you understand the feedback better and shows you're engaged and committed to improving.

Feedback in Different Relationships

Tailoring your feedback approach depending on the relationship is crucial. How you provide feedback to a family member, for example, will differ from how you handle a professional colleague. With family, it's often more personal. It can be more direct, while in the workplace, it needs to be handled with professionalism and a certain level of formality. Understanding the dynamics of each relationship helps deliver feedback most effectively. Keep it light and constructive in social settings, focusing more on positive reinforcements. In professional environments, balance positivity with constructive critiques, ensuring you're clear about expectations and outcomes.

Creating a Culture of Feedback

Imagine a workplace where feedback is as normal as the morning coffee run—where everyone is continually learning, growing, and evolving through regular feedback exchanges. Creating this culture starts with leadership. When leaders openly give and receive feedback, it sets a tone for the entire organization. Encourage regular feedback sessions, make them a part of the routine, and watch as they transform the atmosphere. It's about fostering an environment where feedback is seen not as a threat but as a valuable tool for personal and collective advancement.

By embracing these principles and techniques, you'll find that giving or receiving feedback becomes less about ego and more about growth. When used wisely, it's a powerful tool that can significantly enhance your interactions and relationships across all areas of life. So, the next time you're gearing up to give feedback, remember that it's not just about pointing out what's wrong—it's about opening a dialogue that leads to improvement. And when receiving feedback, see it as an opportunity to refine your skills and grow. It's all part of the journey toward becoming your best self.

As we wrap up this exploration of advanced communication skills, from the finesse of persuasion and negotiation to the depths of empathy and the transformative power of storytelling, remember that each skill enhances how you communicate, connect, and thrive in relationships. Up next, we venture into the realm of maintaining and deepening these connections, ensuring that the bridges built through effective communication are well-maintained and robust. Let's continue to turn the pages, learning and growing together in the art of communication.

MAKE A DIFFERENCE WITH YOUR REVIEW

"You can make more friends in two months by becoming interested in other people than you can in two years by trying to get other people interested in you."

DALE CARNEGIE

People who help others without expecting anything in return live happier and longer lives. So, if we can do that together, I'm all in!

To make that happen, I have a question for you...

Would you help someone you've never met, even if you never got credit for it?

Who is this person, you ask? They are like you. Or, at least, like you used to be. They want to make a difference, they need help, but they're not sure where to start.

Our mission is to make "The Power of Connection" accessible to everyone. Everything we do comes from that mission. And the only way to accomplish it is by reaching... well... everyone. This is where you come in. Most people do, in fact, judge a book by its cover (and its reviews). So here's my ask on behalf of all the people you've never met who are trying to improve their lives:

Please help that person get ahead in life by leaving this book a review.

Your gift costs no money and takes less than sixty seconds, but it can change a person's life forever. Your review could help...

- ...one more person transform their life
- ...one more dream come true
- ...one more person find that missing friend
- ...a fellow reader find the right guide for a more connected life

To get that "feel-good" feeling and help this person for real, all you have to do is... and it takes less than sixty seconds... leave a review. Simply scan the QR code below to leave your review:

If you feel good about helping a faceless person trying to improve their life, you are my kind of person. Welcome to the club. You're one of us.

I'm that much more excited to help you live your best life as quickly and meaningfully as possible. You'll love the lessons and strategies I'm about to share in the coming chapters.

Thank you from the bottom of my heart. Now, back to our regularly scheduled programming.

Your biggest fan,

Liam Grant

CHAPTER 6
SPECIAL SOCIAL
SITUATIONS

A h, special social situations—those delightful moments when you get to put your everyday social skills to the test and either soar like an eagle or ... well, let's say, not soar. The thrilling yet sometimes awkward dance where you put your best foot forward and hope not to step on any toes. Much like networking events, where you navigate a sea of potential mentors, industry leaders, and peers. Dating involves its own set of strategies and charms. But did you know that the skills you hone in business can also work wonders in your personal life? That's right—the art of networking isn't just about exchanging business cards and LinkedIn invites; it's also a powerful tool for building meaningful connections in all areas of life.

In the chapter ahead, we'll explore how mastering the delicate balance of strategy and authenticity in networking can enhance your professional and personal relationships. Whether you're attending a corporate mixer or a social gathering, the principles of making genuine connections, engaging with intent, and leaving a lasting impression are universal. We'll explore how to seamlessly integrate your professional networking skills into your dating life, helping you meet new people, foster deeper relationships, and perhaps even find someone special. So, let's get ready to navigate both the boardroom and the ballroom with confidence and charm. Let's dive in!

Among these, networking events stand out as the gladiator arenas of the social world. Here, you're thrown into a mix of potential mentors, industry leaders, and peers while trying to leave a mark without spilling your drink. So, how do you navigate this maze of handshakes and business cards like a pro? Let's dive right into the art of networking with strategy, authenticity, and maybe a little bit of charm.

NETWORKING LIKE A PRO: BUILDING MEANINGFUL CONNECTIONS

Strategic Approach to Networking

First, walking into a networking event without a plan is like going grocery shopping hungry without a list—you end up with a random assortment of items (or contacts) that might not even make a good meal (or make sense for your career). To avoid this, having a clear strategy is crucial. Start by setting specific goals for each event. Ask yourself, "What do I want to achieve?" Whether meeting three potential mentors or gathering insights on a new industry trend, having these objectives will guide your interactions and help keep you on track.

But it's not just about whom you meet; it's also about how you engage with them. Quality trumps quantity every time. It's better to have meaningful conversations with a few key people than to flit around the room, handing out business cards like they're free samples. Think of each conversation as a mini interview where both sides gauge mutual interest and value. This focused approach makes the experience less overwhelming and increases the chances of forming connections that matter.

Elevator Pitch Refinement

Now, about that infamous elevator pitch—your 30-second window to make a memorable impression. This isn't just rattling off your resume; it's about crafting a narrative highlighting your professional background and goals in a way that captivates and resonates. Start with the basics: who you are, what you do, and what you're passionate about. Then, tailor this pitch to align with your networking goals and your audience's interests.

Consider this: "I'm Alex, a digital marketer with a knack for turning data into compelling brand stories. Currently, I'm exploring opportunities to bring these skills to the tech industry, where innovation meets user engagement." This pitch is concise and specific and opens doors to deeper discussions about tech and marketing. Practice your pitch like you'd practice a key presentation—after all, it often serves as the opening line of your professional introduction.

Fostering Genuine Relationships

Remember, networking isn't a hit-and-run game. The goal is to build genuine, lasting professional relationships. This means follow-up is vital. After each event, reach out with personalized messages to those you connected with. A quick note recalling a specific part of your conversation shows you were genuinely engaged: "Hi Sam, I really enjoyed our chat about innovative education technologies at yesterday's event. As we discussed, I'd love to get your insights on applying these in nonprofit contexts."

Authenticity is your best friend here. Let your professional interactions reflect your genuine interest and integrity. It's about building bridges, not just collecting contacts. Relationships nurtured with sincerity and respect tend to open doors to collaborations, opportunities, and even mentorships that can significantly shape your career trajectory.

Networking Tools and Technology

In today's digital age, networking extends beyond the event itself. Platforms like

LinkedIn are invaluable for pre-event strategies and post-event follow-ups. Before an event, you can use LinkedIn to research attendees and companies of interest. This prep work can help you tailor your conversations and pitches more effectively. After the event, LinkedIn is great for maintaining the connections you've made. Regular updates, sharing relevant articles, and engaging with posts by your new contacts keep you on their radar and foster ongoing interaction.

Interactive Element: Elevator Pitch Builder

Here's a quick exercise to help you refine your elevator pitch: Fill in the blanks: I am [name], a [your profession] who specializes in [your specialty]. I am currently looking for [type of opportunities or goals] in [industry]. Practice this template until your pitch feels natural and compelling. Remember, the goal is to intrigue and invite further conversation, not to close a deal on the spot.

Networking like a pro is about more than just schmoozing and exchanging business cards. It's about strategic preparation, engaging authentically, and using tools to maximize your efforts before, during, and after events. With these strategies in your arsenal, each networking opportunity becomes a stepping stone to new professional landscapes. So, gear up, get out there, and start building those connections that could shape your career trajectory!

FIRST DATE CONVERSATIONS: DOS AND DON'TS

First dates—the perfect mix of excitement and nerves, like stepping onto a rollercoaster or trying a bizarre new ice cream flavor. Will it be thrillingly sweet or just leave a weird taste in your mouth? Much depends on the conversation—that dance of words where you step on each other's toes or glide smoothly across the dance floor. So, how do you ensure your verbal tango feels more like a smooth waltz and less like a clumsy shuffle? Let's unpack some savvy tips for first-date conversations that can turn a nerve-wracking setup into a chance for genuine connection.

Conversation Starters and Topics

Picking suitable topics on a first date is like choosing your playlist for a road trip: the right mix can turn a routine journey into an epic adventure. Start with safe, engaging topics that invite sharing and reflection without diving into the deep end of personal or controversial subjects. Think passions and interests over politics and exes. A good opener could be, "So, what's one book or movie that resonated with you recently?" Their answer, I'm sure, would be, *The Power of Connection*, of course. Okay, maybe not, but this is a simple yet open-ended question, encouraging your date to share something meaningful, and it gives you insights into their tastes and personality.

Travel is another great topic that can open many conversational doors without prying into too personal territories. Asking, "What's the most memorable place you've visited?" can lead to stories and shared experiences. It's also a fantastic way to gauge their adventurous spirit. Food, too, is a universal connector. Inquire about a favorite cuisine or a memorable dining experience. This can seamlessly lead to suggesting a second date at a restaurant serving the cuisine you've just been raving about together.

Reading and Respecting Boundaries

Navigating the unspoken yet crucial boundaries of a first-date conversation is an art. It's about reading both verbal and nonverbal cues. You're on the right track if your date leans in, smiles, and responds enthusiastically. But if they pull back, cross their arms, or give terse replies, you might have tread into no-go territory or picked a topic they're not too keen on.

Respecting these boundaries is critical. If you sense any discomfort, tactfully shift gears. It could be as simple as switching from personal anecdotes to more neutral ground, like discussing a popular new TV series or upcoming local events. The key is to keep the conversation flowing but steer it according to the comfort levels that your date expresses, ensuring that the dialogue remains a two-way street. No one wants to be stuck listening to your monologue about that one time you got lost in IKEA for three hours. Not that I would know anything about that.

Balancing Talking and Listening

A first date should be a dialogue, not a monologue. Striking a balance between talking and listening is crucial. You want to share enough about yourself to pique your date's interest but not so much that your date becomes a spectator to your one-person show. Similarly, be an active listener. This means really hearing what they're saying, not just planning your next anecdote while they speak. Show interest through your body language—nod, smile, and maintain eye contact. Reflect on what you've heard to show you're engaged: "That sounds like an amazing trip! What did you love most about Japan?"

Handling Sensitive Topics

Even with the best intentions, sensitive topics can pop up. Maybe your date mentions a recent breakup in passing, or a political opinion slips out. Handling these moments with tact and grace is crucial. First, gauge whether it's a passing comment or something they're opening up about. If it's the latter, acknowledge their feelings without diving too deep: "It sounds like that was a significant time for you." If it's a controversial topic, acknowledge their viewpoint and gently redirect: "I can see you're passionate about that. I haven't thought about it that deeply, but I'd love to hear more about your travels." Because, let's be honest, debating politics on a first date is like playing with fireworks indoors—it's bound to blow up in your face.

Navigating first-date conversations doesn't have to feel like a minefield. With engaging topics, attentive listening, and respectful boundary navigation, what starts as cautious small talk can blossom into a meaningful connection. So, take a deep breath, arm yourself with these conversational tips, and turn that first date into a promising beginning. Who knows? This could be the start of something wonderful—or, at the very least, a fun story to share at your next gathering. Like the time you debated pineapple on pizza with a near stranger.

NAVIGATING FAMILY GATHERINGS SUCCESSFULLY

Ah, family gatherings—where the turkey isn't the only thing that gets roasted. Whether it's Thanksgiving, a birthday, or just an impromptu barbecue, these occasions can sprinkle a bit of drama on your mashed potatoes if you're unprepared. Setting realistic expectations and having a game plan can transform potential family feuds into a festival of fondness—or at least prevent you from hiding in the bathroom all evening.

Preparation and Expectations

First, let's talk about setting the scene in your mind before you even step into Grandma's house. Know the cast of characters —Uncle Joe, who loves to debate; Aunt Mary, who asks about your dating life as if she's running your Tinder account; and your cousin, who has turned every family event into a conspiracy theory seminar. By anticipating the personalities and potential friction points, you can prepare yourself mentally and emotionally. It's not about expecting the worst; it's about being prepared so you can handle whatever comes your way with grace and humor.

Now, plan your strategies. If political discussions are a minefield, have a few neutral conversation changers ready. Think fun topics like new technology, holiday plans, or the latest movies. These can be lifesavers when you see the conversation veering into dangerous territory. Also, set personal boundaries on topics you're uncomfortable with. Decide in advance how you'll kindly but firmly shift away from unwanted inquiries or debates. It might be something like, "I'm really trying to focus on the positive this year, so I'd love to talk about the good things we've all experienced." Setting these expectations for yourself helps you steer the gathering in a more pleasant direction.

Communication Strategies with Relatives

Navigating the diverse personalities at family gatherings requires a mix of diplomacy and sincerity. Start with the basics: active listening. Even if Uncle Joe passionately explains why his football team is the best, showing genuine interest can keep the peace. It makes the speaker feel valued and heard, paving the way for smoother interactions.

Adapt your communication style to match the relative you're engaging with. For the overly curious Aunt Mary, give answers that satisfy her curiosity without divulging too much. You might say, "I'm enjoying life and learning a lot right now," which gives her something without inviting further prying. For the argumentative cousin, affirm his feelings without stoking the flames. A response like, "That's an interesting point, but I haven't seen it that way," acknowledges their view without escalating the debate.

Dealing with Controversial Topics

It's almost a rule that one controversial topic will pop up between the appetizers and desserts. Steering these conversations requires a gentle touch and a bit of cunning. Redirecting is your first line of defense. If politics comes up, redirect to a personal experience that's related but safer, like a recent volunteer experience or a funny travel story that happened during a voting trip. If the topic persists, mediation might be necessary. Acknowledge each side's views and suggest a neutral observer's compromise, or, better yet, propose discussing it later and moving on to another topic. Sometimes, breaking the pattern with an interjection like, "Hey, let's table this debate—has everyone seen the latest episode of [popular TV show]?" can diffuse tension and redirect attention.

Inclusivity in Family Events

Finally, ensuring everyone feels included can make or break a family gathering. Scan the room—is someone being left out of conversations? Is a new family member looking a bit lost? Bringing them into the fold can make a huge difference. Share a story or ask their opinion on something benign, like food or entertainment. For kids and teens, make sure there are activities or topics they can contribute to. It could be setting up a gaming console where they can play or asking them about their hobbies and interests.

Creating an inclusive atmosphere makes the event more enjoyable for everyone and builds stronger family bonds. It's about ensuring everyone leaves smiling and, hopefully, looking forward to the next gathering. So, as you step into your next family event armed with these strategies, remember that the goal isn't just to survive but to ensure everyone, including yourself, has a good time. After all, family gatherings are about building memories, not stress. So, take a deep breath, put on your game face, and dive into the fray with a plan to make it a gathering for the books! And if all else fails, mention dessert. It's hard to argue when you're enjoying pie.

SOCIAL SKILLS FOR WORKPLACE SUCCESS

Navigating the corporate jungle can sometimes feel less like a walk in the park and more like a tightrope walk over a pool of sharks. But fear not! You can survive and thrive in the workplace with some savvy social skills. Let's break down the essentials of workplace etiquette, building rapport, communicating effectively in team settings, and handling conflicts like a pro.

Professional Decorum and Etiquette

First off, let's talk etiquette. Think of workplace etiquette as the unwritten rules of the office—it's about more than just saying your please and thank yous. It starts with the basics, like dressing appropriately. Whether your office is suit-and-tie formal or more "anything goes," dressing suitably shows respect for your workplace and the people you work with. And here's a tip: Err on the side of caution when in doubt. It's better to be slightly overdressed than to turn up looking like you've mistaken the boardroom for the beach.

Punctuality is another pillar of professional etiquette. Being on time isn't just about clocking in and out; it's about respecting your time and others'. It sends a message that you value the work and the people you work with. My dad's favorite saying about time was, "Five minutes early is on time, on time is late, and late is unforgivable."

Unforgivable might be harsh, but the sentiment is there. And let's remember the golden rule of the modern workplace: managing your digital presence. This means using technology wisely—keeping your phone silent during meetings, being mindful of what you post on social media, and, yes, even resisting the urge to browse through your feed during work hours. These small actions contribute to a professional demeanor that can set you apart in the best way possible.

Building Rapport with Colleagues

Moving on to rapport, consider it the glue that holds workplace relationships together. Building solid relationships with your colleagues doesn't just make your daily grind more enjoyable; it opens doors to new opportunities and collaborations. Start simple. Share a coffee break with a co-worker or ask about their weekend plans. Showing interest in their life outside of work can turn casual colleagues into allies. And when celebrating their professional or personal milestones, a little recognition goes a long way. A congratulatory note for a promotion or a small gesture on their birthday can cement your goodwill and strengthen your workplace bonds.

Effective Communication in Team Settings

In team meetings or collaborations, transparent and respectful communication is key. It's like being an orchestra conductor—every instrument needs to be in tune. Start by setting an agenda and objectives for meetings to ensure everyone is on the same page. During discussions, encourage openness and respect for differing opinions. Make it a point to actively listen—hearing what others are saying, not just waiting for your turn to speak. And remember, feedback is a two-way street; it should be constructive and aimed at solutions, not just pointing out problems. This approach enhances team dynamics and fosters an environment where creativity and cooperation flourish.

Handling Workplace Conflicts

Finally, let's tackle the tricky business of conflict resolution. Conflicts are inevitable wherever there's more than one person, so the key is in how you handle them. Start by staying calm and objective. Approach conflicts as a problem to be solved, not a battle to be won. Mediation skills can be invaluable here—facilitate discussions that allow all parties to express their views and work toward a mutually acceptable solution. Always focus on the issue, not the person, and seek compromise where possible. Remember, the goal is resolution, not escalation. By managing conflicts constructively, you contribute to a healthier, more productive workplace environment. Channel your inner diplomat and leave the drama for reality TV.

Mastering these social skills can make your workplace not just a place where you work but a place where you thrive. Remember, you spend a considerable chunk of your life at work. Why wouldn't you try everything you could to make it a place you enjoy going to every day? From dressing right to managing conflicts, each skill enhances your professional image and ability to work effectively with others. So, the next time you step into your office, remember these tips and watch as you navigate your workday with confidence and finesse. You may even enjoy your day at work. After all, if you spend forty hours a week somewhere, it might as well be a place that doesn't make you want to hide in the supply closet.

HANDLING SOCIAL SITUATIONS IN DIVERSE CULTURAL CONTEXTS

Navigating the complexities of global cultures is like being an explorer in a vast, bustling market, where every turn offers a new color, flavor, or melody. Understanding and respecting cultural differences isn't just about avoiding faux pas; it's about enriching your social toolkit and turning every interaction into a chance to broaden your horizons. So, how do you become a savvy cultural navigator? Let's unpack the essentials of thriving in diverse cultural settings, from decoding traditions to adapting your communication style.

First up, understanding cultural diversity is crucial. Every culture has its own set of unwritten rules—norms, traditions, and ways of communication that shape social interactions. Whether mingling at an international conference or attending a friend's wedding in a foreign country, awareness of these cultural nuances can make the difference between a social blunder and a meaningful exchange. For example, while a firm handshake is expected in many Western cultures, it might be seen as aggressive in Japan, where a bow is the norm. Similarly, while direct eye contact is appreciated in the

USA as a sign of confidence and honesty, it can be considered confrontational in some Asian cultures. Recognizing these differences is the first step in navigating the complex world of cultural interactions.

Developing cultural sensitivity and awareness is next. It's about doing your homework before diving into new cultural waters. A bit of research can go a long way—read up on the dos and don'ts of the culture, learn a few polite phrases in the local language, and understand the basic etiquette. Asking respectful questions is also a key part of developing cultural sensitivity. It shows your interest and willingness to learn rather than assume. For instance, if you're unsure about the appropriate greeting or dress code at a cultural event, asking a knowledgeable friend or host can help you navigate the situation gracefully. Being mindful of cultural dos and don'ts enables you to avoid missteps but also demonstrates respect for the traditions and values of others, paving the way for smoother and more enjoyable interactions.

Adapting your communication style to fit different cultural contexts is where you put your learning into action. Each culture has its own nuances in communication styles— some may value directness and clarity. In contrast, others might prefer more subtle and indirect ways of expressing thoughts. For example, in many Western cultures, being straightforward and to the point is seen as a virtue. In contrast, in many Asian cultures, preserving harmony and avoiding confrontation are often more valued, requiring a more nuanced and careful way of phrasing your thoughts. Adapting your style to these differences doesn't mean changing who you are; it's about adjusting your sails to navigate the winds of cultural diversity more effectively. This adaptability can lead to more meaningful exchanges and prevent misunderstandings arising from cultural misinterpretations.

Finally, every interaction in a diverse cultural setting is a learning opportunity. Embrace these experiences with an open mind and a curious heart. Every conversation is a window into a new world— a chance to learn about different life experiences, viewpoints, and wisdom. These interactions are about expanding your social circle and enriching your understanding of the world. They allow you to see the world through different lenses, enhancing your empathy and broadening your perspective. This openness to learning and adapting enriches your personal growth and deepens your appreciation for the richness of human diversity.

Navigating social situations in diverse cultural contexts is an exhilarating part of the modern social experience. It challenges you to learn, adapt, and embrace the vast array of human expressions and interactions. By understanding cultural diversity, developing sensitivity, adapting your communication style, and viewing each interaction as a learning opportunity, you equip yourself with the tools to survive and thrive in the global social arena. So, step into this vibrant market of cultures with confidence and curiosity, ready to explore, learn, and connect. Just remember to pack your sense of humor and your willingness to adapt because every adventure is better with a smile and a bit of flexibility.

As this chapter closes, we've equipped you with the essentials for handling special social situations, from networking like a pro to navigating complex family dynamics and mastering diverse cultural interactions. These skills are about making it through social events and turning each interaction into an opportunity for personal growth and meaningful connections. Ready to continue the adventure? In the next chapter, we dive deeper into developing and sustaining individual and professional relationships because excellent social skills are the foundation for lasting relationships.

CHAPTER 7
DEVELOPING
RELATIONSHIPS

E ver feel like making friends should come with a manual? Like, "Congratulations on your new acquaintance! Here are three easy steps to upgrade to a friendship." Well, buckle up because this chapter is pretty much that manual—minus the overly optimistic three-step promise. It's all about diving deep into the art of turning those "Hey, how's it going?" interactions into "Hey, you'll never believe what happened!" friendships.

DEEPENING FRIENDSHIPS: BEYOND ACQUAINTANCES

Identifying Potential Friendships

Let's start with the basics—identifying which acquaintances could become your next BFF. This isn't about crafting a mysterious friendship potion but spotting the right ingredients. First up, common interests. These are the spices of friendship—a shared love for books, yoga, hiking, or an unhealthy obsession with reality TV can form the initial bond. Look for signs during conversations or check their social media to see what hobbies or passions light them up. I know what you're thinking. Do you want me to stalk my possible future friends? Well, yeah! I mean, no … Well, continue reading.

Next, mutual respect. This is the yeast that makes the friendship rise (without it, things can fall flat really fast). It's visible when they value your opinions, even if they differ, and when there's a mutual effort to understand and support each other. Lastly, the potential for reciprocal support—this is the sugar of the relationship. It's sweet when it's balanced. Does this person celebrate your successes? Are they there when you're in a jam? If you find yourself nodding along, then hey, you might just have found a friendship candidate.

Investing Time and Effort

Don't expect this friendship to grow from a seedling to a mighty oak overnight. Investing time and effort is crucial. Regular communication is your water here—check in often, make plans, and don't let those "Let's catch up soon" promises become relics. Shared experiences are the sunshine; they help strengthen the bonds. Whether trying out a new restaurant, hiking, or attending a concert, these activities build memories and deepen connections. Remember, the more positive energy you invest, the stronger the friendship grows. If all else fails, bribe them with snacks—no one can resist snacks.

Vulnerability and Sharing

Here comes the tricky part—vulnerability. Yes, it can feel like doing a trust fall with your eyes closed, but it's a powerful way to deepen emotional bonds. Start small. Share a personal story or a challenge you're facing and see how they respond. Suppose they meet your openness with empathy and their own share of individual thoughts. In that case, you've got the green light to gradually open up more. This mutual sharing creates a safe space where roots of trust grow.

Maintaining and Nurturing Friendships

Keeping a friendship thriving requires more than just occasional watering; it needs consistent care. Remembering important events like birthdays or cheering them on during significant life moments shows you care. Acts of appreciation, no matter how small—like sending a congratulatory message or a thoughtful gift—can mean a lot. And let's not forget support during rough patches. Being there when things get rocky— offering a listening ear or a helping hand —cements a friendship like nothing else. These moments reinforce the "through thick and thin" bond. Plus, it's always handy to have a friend who knows where all the bodies are buried (figuratively, of course).

Interactive Element: Friendship Journaling Prompt

To help you apply these insights, here's a little exercise. Grab a journal and jot down the names of a few acquaintances you think could become closer friends. For each person, write down what common interests you share (here's where that social media stalking comes in handy), examples of mutual respect, and how you've supported each other so far. This reflection helps you identify potential deep friendships and sets a clear path on how to develop them. So, what are you waiting for? Start turning those acquaintances into lifelong friends!

By understanding the crucial steps of identifying potential friends, investing time and effort, opening up through vulnerability, and maintaining these relationships, you're well on your way to enriching your social landscape. Remember, every deep friendship was once just an acquaintance. With a little effort and a lot of heart, who knows how many amazing people are waiting to journey with you from a simple "hello" to a profound "you mean the world to me?" Now, let's keep these good vibes rolling and turn the page to discover more about nurturing these connections.

STRATEGIES FOR LONG-DISTANCE RELATIONSHIPS

Long-distance relationships are like maintaining your fitness level while only visiting the gym via video call—challenging but definitely doable with the right strategies. So, how do you keep the love boat sailing smoothly when you're in one time zone and your significant other is in another? Well, it's all about mastering the art of communication, setting realistic expectations, keeping things fresh, and handling the inevitable bumps along the road.

Communication Plans

First up, let's talk about crafting a solid communication plan. Think of this as your relationship's backbone—it must be strong and flexible. With the buffet of tech options available, from instant messaging and video calls to good old emails (yes, they're still a thing), you've got tools to stay connected. But here's the kicker: it's not just what tools you use; it's how you use them. Aligning these tools with both your schedules and lifestyles is crucial. If your partner is a night owl and you're up with the larks, agree on when you're both alert and can truly engage. Maybe a video call over coffee in the morning or a late-night chat session works for you two. The key is consistency and respect for each other's time—no one likes feeling like they're squeezing into someone else's to-do list.

Switch things up occasionally to keep the communication dynamic. A spontaneous love note through a text or an e-card saying "thinking of you" can make your partner's day. These little surprises keep the emotional connection lively. And let's not forget the power of voice—sometimes, a quick phone call can communicate more warmth and affection than a dozen texts. And hey, there's nothing like leaving a goofy voicemail to remind them why they miss you!

Managing Expectations

Setting realistic expectations is the frame that supports the picture of your relationship. It's about knowing what's achievable and not setting yourself up for disappointment. Be clear about how often you can visit each other. If jet-setting every weekend isn't on your bingo card, thanks to budget or job constraints, aim for a monthly rendezvous or plan a longer stay every few months. Discuss what each of you expects in terms of daily communication, too. Does a good morning text set the right tone for your day, or are you okay with catching up in detail every few days? Transparent conversations about these topics prevent feelings of neglect or frustration arising from mismatched expectations.

Keeping the Connection Alive

Now for the fun part—keeping the relationship vibrant and exciting. Think of your relationship as a canvas where both of you get to throw on colors that reflect your personality. Engage in activities that can be shared from a distance. Start a book club for two, where you read and discuss the same book during your calls.

Watch a movie simultaneously and share your reactions via chat. Or embark on a "fitness challenge together" where you motivate each other and share progress. These shared experiences create common ground and give you new things to discuss, keeping the relationship dynamic and engaging.

And who says dates are only for those who can physically meet? Set up a virtual date night—cook the same meal in your separate kitchens, set the ambiance with some music, and enjoy dinner together over video chat. These moments can make the distance feel slightly less daunting and remind you why you're putting in the effort. And if you're both terrible cooks, it makes for a great story to laugh about later.

Handling Challenges and Conflicts

Handling challenges and conflicts with grace and understanding is crucial.

Misunderstandings can be more frequent when most communication happens through screens, which lack the full range of nonverbal cues. When issues arise, address them directly. Don't let resentment build up. Be honest about your feelings, and invite your partner to share their perspective. Practicing active listening during these conversations helps ensure you both feel heard and valued. And if all else fails, remember that emojis were invented to fill those emotional gaps. Just go easy on the eggplant and peach ones!

Feelings of loneliness or dealing with the stress of reunions, where you might feel pressure for everything to be perfect, are common in long-distance relationships. Acknowledge these feelings openly and discuss them with your partner. Find ways to support each other through these emotions. Sometimes, knowing you're not navigating these challenges alone can make all the difference.

Long-distance relationships require effort, no doubt, but with a robust plan for communication, realistic expectations, creative ways to stay connected, and strategies to handle challenges, you can maintain a strong, healthy relationship, even across miles. So, keep your hearts tuned to the same frequency, and watch how distance can teach you a thing or two about love, resilience, and the art of staying connected. Who knows, by the time you finally close the distance, you'll have the kind of relationship skills that make you the envy of all your friends.

FOSTERING TRUST AND HONESTY IN RELATIONSHIPS

Trust is the glue that holds any relationship together, be it with your best buddy, partner, or dog (yes, Fido needs to trust you won't steal his treats). But building this trust isn't about grand gestures or solemn promises—it's about the simple, consistent actions that show you're reliable, day in and day out. Think of trust like a brick wall you're building—every consistent action you take is like adding another brick. Whether it's always being truthful about your whereabouts or following through on your promises, these bits of consistency add up. They show that you can be counted on, making the foundation of your relationship as solid as a rock.

For instance, let's say you've promised to help your friend move on Saturday. If you flake out, that's a brick removed from your wall of trust. But if you show up, maybe even with coffee for the crew, you've not only added a brick but perhaps some lovely decorative stonework as well. Over time, these consistent actions create a robust structure of trust. And it's not just about the big promises— it's the little things, too. Answering texts promptly, being punctual for meet-ups, and listening attentively when they talk about their day—all these actions signal that you respect and value the relationship.

Now, on to the part about being as open as a book (or at least a magazine). Honest communication is the open door that leads to trust. It's about being transparent and upfront about your feelings and concerns without turning the conversation into a blame game. Say you're feeling sidelined because your friend has been MIA since they started dating someone new. Instead of bottling up those feelings until you explode like a shaken soda, choose a calm moment to express yourself. Use "I" statements that focus on your feelings rather than accusing. Something like, "I've been feeling left out since we haven't hung out much. Maybe we could set up a weekly coffee date?" This approach opens the door for honest dialogue without putting them on the defensive.

But what happens when that trust is breached? Maybe a secret was spilled, or a critical commitment was broken. Rebuilding trust is akin to fixing a cracked sculpture—it's possible. Still, the repair will always show if not done carefully. Start with accountability. Owning up to your part in the breach shows maturity and sincerity. Next up: forgiveness. This isn't about excusing the behavior but about letting go of its hold on you and the relationship. Now for the repair work—open dialogue about what went wrong and how to prevent it in the future sets the stage for rebuilding trust. Regular check-ins on feelings and boundaries can help ensure the relationship is healing correctly. Think of it as relationship maintenance, like changing your car's oil before the engine seizes up.

Preventative measures are like weatherproofing for your trust wall. Clear boundaries are essential—know where the lines are that shouldn't be crossed. Regular, open communication keeps everything transparent, and shared goals can keep you both aligned on where you're heading. Just like you wouldn't let the roof of your house go without maintenance, don't let your relationship suffer from neglect. Regular check-ins on how you're both feeling can catch small cracks before they become gaping holes.

In any relationship, fostering trust and honesty is less about the occasional grand gesture and more about the daily, consistent practices that show you care and respect each other. The steady drip fills the bucket, the repeated hammering that builds the house. So keep laying those bricks of trust, keep that door of communication wide open, and watch your relationships grow stronger and more resilient, ready to withstand the tests of time. And remember, even if your trust wall gets a little shaky, you can always add more bricks—just make sure they come with a side of coffee.

BALANCING PROFESSIONAL AND PERSONAL RELATIONSHIPS

Navigating the tightrope between your professional and personal lives can sometimes feel like you're a circus performer, except without the safety net. It's about maintaining your cool when your worlds collide—like not letting slip that embarrassing nickname your siblings call you during a board meeting. Setting clear boundaries is your first line of defense. These are the invisible fences that help everyone know where the yard ends. It's essential to decide early on what you are willing to share and what stays off-limits, especially when your colleagues start feeling like friends. Communicating these boundaries effectively is like setting up clear, visible, and respectful signposts. For instance, if you're uncomfortable discussing your dating life at work, a simple "I prefer keeping my personal life out of the workplace" should help colleagues respect your space.

Now, on to the juggling act—time management. Ensuring that your professional and personal relationships get the attention they deserve requires serious prioritization skills. Start by assessing how much time you can dedicate to each area without feeling like you've cloned yourself. Use tools like digital calendars for work meetings and scheduling time with family and friends. And yes, sometimes you must pencil in "me time," too. Prioritizing isn't about consistently choosing work over family or friends; it's about making informed choices each day based on what needs your attention most.

Maybe it's your daughter's piano recital today and a client presentation tomorrow. Balancing isn't about always keeping the scales even but adjusting as you go.

The waters can get murky when your professional and personal lives overlap, such as working with a close friend or hiring a family member. It's like mixing chocolate with … well, more chocolate. Sounds great but can be too much. To avoid conflicts of interest, transparency is critical. Be upfront about your relationships with colleagues and superiors to sidestep any potential bias accusations. Establish clear professional guidelines with your friend or relative. Just because you share Thanksgiving dinner doesn't mean they get a free pass on deadlines. This distinction helps keep your professional credibility intact and ensures that personal relationships don't cloud your professional judgments.

Maintaining professionalism is crucial, especially when personal relationships are in the mix. It's easy to let your guard down and become too casual, but remember, the office isn't your living room. Upholding professional standards in communication, conduct, and confidentiality helps draw the line. For instance, refrain from sharing that hilarious but inappropriate meme with your co-worker because you've hung out at a few barbecues.

Keeping these spheres distinct helps prevent situations where personal feelings might influence professional decisions, ensuring decisions are made based on merit, not emotions.

You create a balanced environment where your careers and personal relationships can thrive by mastering the art of setting clear boundaries, managing your time effectively, navigating overlaps between personal and professional lives with integrity, and maintaining unwavering professionalism. So, whether you're scheduling a meeting or a family dinner, remember that it's all about knowing where to draw the line and when to cross it carefully.

Rekindling Old Friendships

Ever stumbled upon an old photo and found yourself smiling, reminiscing about the good old days with a friend you haven't spoken to in ages? It's like finding a forgotten song that used to be a hit on your personal chart. Rekindling an old friendship can feel like trying to revive that hit song on modern airwaves—both exciting and a tad daunting. But fear not; with a bit of finesse and sincerity, you can bring back the magic of old friendships just like a classic vinyl making a comeback.

Reaching Out to Reconnect

Initiating contact after a long silence requires a delicate balance of warmth and respect for their current situation. It's important to acknowledge the time that has passed without making the conversation feel like a guilt trip. A simple, heartfelt message can open the doors: "Hey [Name], I stumbled upon some pictures of us from back in the day, and it got me thinking about how much fun we had together. I'd love to catch up and hear about what's new with you!" It's light and breezy and places the ball in their court without imposing any obligations. Remember, the tone of your message can set the stage for renewed friendship or remind them why you drifted apart. So keep it cheerful and nostalgic, yet respectful of their current life.

Addressing Past Conflicts

If your friendship faded on a less-than-perfect note, tackling past conflicts with a mature and forgiving attitude can pave the way for sincere reconciliation. Approach this delicately; rehashing old wounds isn't the goal. Instead, focus on mutual forgiveness and the desire to move forward. You might say, "I know we didn't part ways on the best terms, and I've always regretted how things went down between us. I would love to make amends and start anew if you're open to it." This shows you're not shirking responsibility and are eager to rebuild on a foundation of mutual respect and understanding. Admitting you were a bit of a knucklehead can be strangely liberating!

Rebuilding the Friendship Foundation

Starting afresh means slowly laying down new planks over the old foundation. Begin with shared memories, as these are your common ground. Reminisce about the good times but be sure to show interest in their current life. Gradually introduce current interests and updates about your life. It's like mixing classic tracks with new ones; you keep the essence but add fresh beats. Engage them with what's happening now but link it back to shared past experiences. "I remember how we used to binge-watch old movies; I recently saw [Movie], and it reminded me of our marathon nights! What are you into these days?"

Maintaining the Rekindled Friendship

Keeping the flame alive requires consistent effort since the sparks are flying again. Unlike new friendships, where everything is a discovery, you're nurturing a grown plant back to health here. Regular communication is vital—texts, calls, or even sharing a meme can keep you connected without being overbearing. Celebrate their successes, provide support during lows, and, most importantly, make new memories. Perhaps plan a meet-up or start a shared hobby. It's about showing you're here for the long haul, not just reliving the glory days.

Rekindling an old friendship is like polishing a cherished piece of furniture that has been gathering dust in the attic. It requires care, effort, and a gentle touch, but the result can be a restored relationship that brings new joy and richness to your life. As you step into the world of renewed friendships, carry with you the lessons of the past and the excitement for future possibilities. And just like that, your social soundtrack gets much richer, filled with the familiar tunes of old friendships dancing to the rhythm of new beginnings.

LEADING INTO THE NEXT CHAPTER

As we wrap up our exploration of rekindling old friendships, we carry forward the theme of nurturing and sustaining the relationships we hold dear. Each connection, whether renewed or newly forged, adds to the intricate fabric of our social lives. Up next, we shift our focus to navigating the complexities of social interactions in various settings, ensuring we're equipped to handle whatever social curveballs life might throw our way. Let's continue to weave strong, vibrant connections that enrich our lives and those around us.

CHAPTER 8
CONFLICT RESOLUTION AND DIFFICULT CONVERSATIONS

Have you ever found yourself in the middle of a squabble over something so trivial that you can't even remember how it started? Maybe it was over who got the last slice of pizza or whose turn it was to walk the dog in the rain. Big and small conflicts are as much a part of our daily lives as forgetting where we put our keys. People my age know the struggle with misplaced keys. But unlike misplaced keys, unresolved conflicts can leave a lingering sense of frustration. Whether it's a spat with a friend or a standoff with a co-worker, knowing how to navigate these choppy waters can turn potential disasters into opportunities for growth and understanding. Buckle up because we're about to dive into the essentials of conflict resolution, turning you into a peacemaking pro!

ESSENTIALS OF CONFLICT RESOLUTION

Understanding Conflict Dynamics

First things first: To understand the beast you're dealing with. Conflict isn't just an annoying hurdle; it's a complex dynamic that can escalate quicker than you can say "misunderstanding." Picture this: What starts as a calm discussion about who should have cleaned the kitchen can quickly spiral into a heated argument about every chore ever overlooked. Suddenly, you're debating who forgot to take out the trash in 2007. This escalation happens because conflicts often trigger our emotional responses before our rational minds have a chance to catch up.

Recognizing the stages of conflict—from a disagreement to a full-blown feud—can help you intervene before things get out of hand. Each stage ups the ante, increasing the emotional heat and reducing the chances of a calm resolution. And here's where roles come into play. Are you the avoider who sidesteps conflict, hoping it'll magically dissolve? Or perhaps the confronter who meets conflicts head-on? Understanding your default role and how it affects the conflict's trajectory can be a game-changer in managing disputes effectively.

Principles of Conflict Resolution

Now, on to the golden rules of conflict resolution. The first rule? Focus on interests, not positions. It's easy to get stuck on staking out a position ("I want the report done by Thursday!") and forget about the underlying interests that are driving it ("I need the report done so I can present it at the meeting on Friday."). By shifting the focus to interests, you open up avenues for understanding and compromise.

Creating options for mutual gain is like looking for a win-win scenario where both parties get something that satisfies their interests. It's not about slicing the pie into ever smaller pieces but about making the pie bigger so everyone feels they've had a decent slice. And who doesn't love a bigger pie? Lastly, ensuring that solutions are based on objective criteria can help take the personal sting out of decisions. Instead of basing decisions on who shouts the loudest, you base them on fair standards that apply equally to everyone involved.

Role of Empathy in Resolution

Empathy, the ability to understand and share the feelings of another, is your secret weapon in resolving conflicts. It moves the situation from a tug-of-war to a collaborative problem-solving session. When you genuinely try to understand the other person's perspective without immediately trying to counter it with your own, you lay down the weapons and start building bridges. It's not about agreeing with them but about acknowledging their feelings and perspectives as valid. This can significantly lower defenses, paving the way for more open and productive discussions.

Resolution Techniques

Regarding the actual resolution, techniques like mediation, negotiation, and facilitated dialogue are your tools of the trade. Mediation involves bringing in a neutral third party to help clarify issues and explore potential solutions. It's like having a referee in a sports game, ensuring that things stay fair and constructive. Negotiation is more about give and-take, where both parties work together to find a solution that meets their essential interests.

Facilitated dialogue is a structured process that helps keep the conversation focused and productive, ensuring that all voices are heard and considered. Knowing when and how to use these techniques can make the difference between a resolution everyone can live with and a festering issue that resurfaces at the next family gathering or team meeting.

So there you have it—a toolkit for tackling conflicts with confidence and savvy. Whether you're dealing with a minor disagreement or a significant dispute, these strategies can help you navigate the stormy seas of human relationships with a little more grace and much less stress. Let's keep these peacemaking vibes going as we explore more about de-escalating tense situations in the next section. Ready to turn down the heat and turn up the understanding? Let's go!

STRATEGIES FOR DE-ESCALATING TENSE SITUATIONS

Have you ever encountered a conversation where the temperature rises faster than a thermometer on a sunny day in Death Valley? You're not alone. Escalating tensions in discussions can sneak up like ninjas—silent but stressful. Recognizing these early signs of a heated conversation can be your first step in putting on the brakes before things go off the rails. Signs like voices inching higher, speech speeding up like a sports commentator at the final goal, or bodies tensing up as if preparing for a duel. When you spot these signals, it's your cue to switch gears.

Maintaining a calm and composed demeanor during these moments is akin to being the cool cucumber in a salad bowl of jalapeños. It's all about self-control. Techniques like controlled breathing can be a lifesaver here. Try inhaling deeply through your nose, holding it for a few seconds, and then exhaling slowly through your mouth. This isn't just a relaxation cliché; it's a physiological hack to calm your nervous system, signaling your body that it's not in fight-or-flight mode. Another trick is the strategic pause. Before you respond, take a brief moment to collect your thoughts. This pause can give you enough time to frame your response in a way that douses flames rather than fuels them.

Now, let's talk about the words you choose. The language of de-escalation is like verbal aloe vera—cooling and soothing. Phrases that acknowledge the other person's feelings can make a world of difference. Try sprinkling in some empathetic statements like, "I see this is really important to you; let's find a way to address it" or "I understand why that upset you." These aren't just niceties; they're tactical tools that show you're on their side—or at least not against them. It's about finding that sweet spot where you both feel understood and are open to finding common ground.

Sometimes, however, the best move is to strategically withdraw. This isn't about storming off in a huff. Instead, think of it as hitting the pause button. Proposing a break, like "Let's take a few minutes to cool down" can be beneficial. It's important to frame this break as a mutual chance for reflection, not an escape route. You might say, "I think we could use a quick break to think things over. Let's regroup in ten?" Timing is crucial here; suggest a pause before reaching the boiling point, not after things have already spilled over.

Navigating tense situations with tact and poise can turn potential conflicts into opportunities for growth and understanding. By keeping your cool, choosing your words wisely, and knowing when to take a step back, you'll manage these moments better and come out looking like the Zen master of conversations. So next time you feel the heat rising, remember these strategies and watch as you transform tension into constructive dialogue, keeping your social interactions as smooth as a well-mixed cocktail.

COMMUNICATING DURING EMOTIONAL UPHEAVALS

Have you ever encountered a heated conversation in which emotions are running high and, suddenly, it feels like you're both speaking different languages? Emotional conversations are like navigating a minefield while blindfolded—you never know when you might step on a trigger and blow everything up. Managing your emotions during these high-stakes talks is crucial, not just for peacekeeping but also for maintaining healthy, resilient relationships. Let's unpack some tried-and-true strategies to keep cool and communicate effectively, even when the emotional alarm bells are ringing.

First off, recognizing your personal triggers is a game-changer. These are the comments, tones, or topics that make your blood pressure soar. Maybe it's when someone dismisses your ideas or you feel unfairly criticized. Whatever sets you off, becoming aware of these triggers is the first step in managing your reactions. Think of it as setting up an early warning system; the sooner you know the alarms might go off, the quicker you can diffuse them. Techniques like journaling your feelings post-conflict or reflecting on past arguments can help you spot patterns in what pushes your buttons. Once you know your triggers, you can brace yourself better or steer conversations away from danger zones.

Now, what about when your emotions have already hijacked the conversation? Here's where self-soothing techniques come into play. Techniques like the 5-4-3-2-1 grounding exercise can work wonders. Notice five things you can see, four you can touch, three you can hear, two you can smell, and one you can taste. This brings your focus back to the present, pulling you away from escalating emotions. Another quick fix? During difficult conversations, have a "stress ball" or a similar tactile object. Squeezing it can help channel some of that emotional energy physically, keeping your verbal responses more measured. Just don't accidentally launch it at the other person—stress balls are for squeezing, not throwing!

Moving on to expressing yourself without turning the conversation into a blame game, the magic lies in the power of "I" statements. Instead of saying, "You never listen to me," try, "I feel overlooked when I speak, and others don't seem to listen." This subtle shift puts the focus on your feelings rather than accusing the other person, which lowers their need to defend themselves and keeps the dialogue open and less combative. Clearly communicating your needs and feelings this way opens doors for understanding, not conflict. It's about being honest about your feelings without making the other person the villain in your story. Remember, you're not auditioning for a soap opera!

Active listening is your bridge over troubled waters. It's about genuinely hearing the other person, not just planning your subsequent counterattack while they speak. This means tuning in with all your senses, acknowledging their feelings, and reflecting on what you hear without immediately interjecting your perspective. For instance, if someone says, "I'm upset because I feel ignored," you might respond, "It sounds like you're feeling really overlooked, and that's hard." This validates their feelings and shows that you're really with them, not against them. It can turn a confrontation into a conversation where both sides feel seen and heard.

Lastly, finding common ground for emotional issues can act like a reset button. It's about discovering shared feelings or goals to help realign the conversation. Say you're arguing about who does more household chores. The common ground might be, "We both feel overwhelmed with tasks and need more downtime." Recognizing this can shift the focus from conflict to cooperation, as you both work toward a mutual goal of balancing chores for more relaxation time. Because, let's face it, nobody's dream weekend involves a chore marathon.

Mastering these strategies transforms emotional upheavals into opportunities for deeper connections and understanding. It's about taking charge of your emotions, communicating with clarity and empathy, and listening in a way that bridges gaps rather than widening them. So, next time you feel a storm brewing in a conversation, remember these tools. With practice, you'll handle emotional talks more effectively and build stronger, more understanding relationships in all areas of your life.

ASSERTIVENESS WITHOUT AGGRESSIVENESS

When we hear the word "assertiveness," it might conjure up images of someone who always gets their way, no matter what. But let's clear the air: being assertive isn't about being pushy or overbearing. It's about communicating clearly and confidently without stepping on others' toes. It's like being your ship's captain without becoming a pirate. Assertiveness is your sweet spot between the passive "whatever you say" and the aggressive "it's my way or the highway." It's about expressing your thoughts, feelings, and needs in a manner that respects your and others' rights.

Now, how do you pull off this balancing act? It starts with your body language. Imagine you're telling a friend they've hurt your feelings. Your message loses weight if you're slumped over or avoiding eye contact. But stand straight, maintain eye contact, and use gestures that indicate confidence without aggression, like open palms or relaxed arms, and you're communicating strength and openness. It's about matching your body language to your words, reinforcing that you mean what you say, and saying it respectfully.

Voice control is another crucial player. Ever noticed how a calm, steady voice can make even harsh words seem less daunting? That's your goal. Keeping your tone even and your volume moderate sends a message of composure and control, which makes others more likely to listen and take you seriously. It's not about being loud—it's about being clear. Think of it as speaking in high definition: every word is crisp, clear, and intentional.

Setting boundaries is where a lot of folks get tripped up. It's one thing to know your limits but communicating them without sounding like a rulebook is another. Start by being clear about what's okay and what's not. For example, saying, "I need to have this weekend to myself; I'm not available to work overtime," sets a clear boundary about your time. It's straightforward and respectful. Make sure to express your boundaries consistently, not just when you've reached your limit. Consistent setting of boundaries helps others understand your needs without you swinging from passive to aggressive.

Handling pushback is the final hurdle in mastering assertiveness. Not everyone will stand up and applaud when you stand up for yourself. You might face resistance or even outright disagreement. Here's where your assertiveness gets tested. Stay consistent— reiterate your boundaries and why they're essential. For instance, if someone continues to ask you to bend a clearly set boundary, a response like, "I understand this is important, but so is my prior commitment. I need to stick with what we agreed on" reaffirms your stance without escalating the situation.

Navigating pushback requires a cocktail of patience, clarity, and firmness. Keep your responses free from sarcasm or defensiveness. Think of it as holding your ground during an earthquake—keep your stance wide and your balance centered. And remember, being assertive means respecting the pushback, too. It's about dialogue, not monologue. Listen to what the other side has to say, and you might find a middle ground that respects both your boundaries and their needs.

Mastering assertiveness without slipping into aggressiveness is like learning a dance. It takes practice, awareness, and quite a bit of stepping on toes until you get it right. But once you do, it's a game-changer. You'll be able to express yourself clearly and confidently while keeping your relationships respectful and intact. So next time you find yourself shrinking back or gearing up for battle, remember: there's a middle path. Walk it with your head held high and your respect for others clear in your stride.

NAVIGATING CRITICISM AND NEGATIVE FEEDBACK

Let's face it: nobody wakes up thinking, "I hope someone critiques my work today!" Yet, criticism, when dished out constructively, can be like that tough-love coach who pushes you to your limits so you can grow. It's not about sugar-coating the pill but delivering it in a digestible and, ultimately, beneficial way. And hey, receiving criticism without throwing a tantrum? That's an art form in and of itself. So, let's unpack how you can both give and receive criticism like a pro, turning potential sore points into springboards for growth.

Handling criticism starts with a mindset adjustment. It's tempting to take negative feedback as a personal attack, but here's a different angle: separate your self-worth from the critique. Imagine your project or behavior as a separate entity standing next to you. Criticism directed at it doesn't diminish your value as a person or professional. View feedback as a flashlight aimed at areas that need improvement, not a spotlight on your faults. This perspective shift is crucial and can transform feedback sessions from defensive battles into learning opportunities.

Now, let's talk about being on the giving end of criticism. The key here is to be specific and focus on behaviors, not personality traits. Saying, "Your report was submitted late, which delayed the team's progress," is far more constructive than, "You're always so disorganized!" The former points out a specific issue and its impact, while the latter could trigger defensiveness and resentment. Always pair criticism with suggestions for improvement. It's like saying, "Here's a hurdle," and then offering a leg up to help them over it. For instance, "Next time, setting a reminder a day ahead could help ensure you meet the deadline."

Maintaining professionalism is your safety net when navigating the slippery slopes of giving and receiving feedback, especially in the workplace, where dynamics can be as complex as assembling IKEA furniture. Those IKEA directions, am I right? Ugh! Keeping interactions respectful and objective helps preserve dignity and trust. It's about keeping calm, choosing your words carefully, and addressing issues promptly and privately. This professional decorum prevents feedback from being tainted with emotional bias or personal grievances, making it more likely to be accepted and acted upon.

Follow-up actions are where you ensure that feedback doesn't just evaporate into thin air. After receiving criticism:

1. Take proactive steps like creating a plan for improvement or seeking further clarification to fully understand the feedback.
2. If you're the one who provided the critique, offer support.
3. Check in to see how they're progressing with the improvements or if they need more resources or guidance.

This shows that you care about their growth and reinforces the constructive nature of your feedback.

Navigating the world of criticism and feedback with grace and effectiveness is about smoothing current issues and paving the way for future interactions. Whether you're on the giving or receiving end, handling feedback well enhances communication, strengthens professional relationships, and fosters a culture of continuous improvement. So next time you face a feedback session, remember: it's not a minefield to tiptoe around but a gold-mine of opportunities to dig into.

WRAPPING UP CHAPTER 8

As we wrap up our journey through the lively terrains of conflict resolution and difficult conversations, remember that the essence of navigating these challenges lies in mastering techniques and maintaining a spirit of growth and empathy. From understanding the dynamics of conflicts to de-escalating tense situations, communicating through emotional upheavals, asserting yourself without aggression, and handling criticism constructively—each skill enriches your ability to interact with understanding and effectiveness. As we turn the page to the next chapter, we carry forward the wisdom of turning adversities into avenues for personal and relational growth. Let's continue to build on these foundations, fostering connections that aren't just resilient but also deeply rewarding.

CHAPTER 9
ENHANCING EMOTIONAL INTELLIGENCE

E ver felt like you're playing an emotional version of pinball, bouncing between feeling pumped, pooped, and perplexed all in one day? Welcome to the world of emotional intelligence (EI), or, as I like to call it, the key that can significantly elevate your social life and career. Think of EI not just as a fancy buzzword but as your inner emotional guide that helps you navigate life's social puzzles and conflicts with finesse and empathy. So, buckle up! Let's dive deep into what EI really is, why it matters, and how you can boost your EI levels without feeling like you're cramming for the world's most challenging exam.

THE BASICS OF EMOTIONAL INTELLIGENCE

Defining Emotional Intelligence

First, understanding EI is about more than getting all academic (no pop quizzes here, I promise). Simply put, EI is your ability to recognize and manage your own emotions, as well as understand and influence the feelings of others. Picture it as having a Swiss army knife for handling emotional challenges. The concept breaks down into five core components: self-awareness, self-regulation, motivation, empathy, and social skills. Each element plays a crucial role in how you perceive, express, develop, and maintain social relationships.

- **Self-Awareness**: This is all about knowing your own emotions. It's like being your own emotional detective; the more clued in you are about what makes you tick, the better you can manage your reactions.
- **Self-Regulation**: Have you figured out your emotions? Great! Can you control them, or do they end up controlling you? That's what self-regulation is all about.
- **Motivation**: This goes beyond just dragging yourself out of bed for work or school. It's about what internally drives you to pursue goals with energy and persistence.
- **Empathy**: This is your ability to understand others' emotions. It's about putting yourself in their shoes without actually taking them. That would be weird and possibly a fashion faux pas.
- **Social Skills**: Last but not least, these are the skills you use to communicate and interact with others effectively. They transform awkward silences into meaningful conversations.

Importance in Social Interactions

Now, why should you care? Because EI is the engine behind your social vehicle. High EI can lead to better relationships at work and home, fewer misunderstandings, and, yes, even a more fulfilling love life. It helps you resolve conflicts without becoming a reality TV show and navigate social gatherings without feeling like a wallflower. In professional settings, EI can be the difference between being seen as a leader or a follower, influencing how you handle team dynamics, leading projects, and getting recognized for promotions.

Assessing Personal EI

So, how do you measure where you stand on the EI scale? Start by taking a hard look at how you react in various emotional situations. Reflect on recent conflicts or emotional exchanges. Were you the cool cucumber or the hothead? Assessing your EI isn't about judging yourself—it's about understanding yourself to pinpoint areas for improvement. Formal assessments like the Emotional Quotient Inventory (EQ-i) or the MayerSalovey-Caruso Emotional Intelligence Test (MSCEIT) can provide more structured insights.

Developing EI Skills

Here's the kicker: EI can be strengthened over time with practice and patience. It's not like height; you don't just reach a point, and that's it. You can always grow emotionally. Start by practicing mindfulness to enhance your self-awareness. Tune into your emotional reactions during the day and ask yourself why you feel a certain way. To boost your empathy, try listening more than you speak in conversations, focusing on understanding the other person's perspective. For social skills, engage in diverse social situations that challenge you to adapt and learn. Enhancing your EI is a journey, not a sprint (and definitely not just another item on your to-do list).

Navigating the complexities of emotions and social interactions with a strong EI can turn everyday challenges into opportunities for personal growth and deeper connections. Whether in a heated boardroom discussion or a heart-to-heart with a friend, your emotional intelligence is the silent superpower that can truly make a difference. So, why not start flexing those emotional muscles?

RECOGNIZING EMOTIONAL TRIGGERS IN SOCIAL INTERACTIONS

Have you ever been chilling? You're totally fine, and then someone says something offhand that sets you off. Suddenly, you're not chill at all. You're as ticked off as a cat slapped with a wet towel. Well, those are your emotional triggers at work, my friend. They're like those sneaky little lines in the sand that you don't see until you've already stepped over them and set off an emotional landmine. Identifying what specific words, actions, or situations trigger your emotional explosions isn't just useful; it's crucial for navigating the social seas without causing a storm. Let's break it down.

Start by playing detective with your own emotions. Next time you find yourself going from zero to sixty on the emotional scale, hit the pause button. Ask yourself, "What just happened?" Was it a comment, a gesture, or a situation? Pinpointing the exact trigger can be like finding the source of a river—all the little streams of reaction lead back to it. This self-observation is your first tool. Reflect on your day or write in a journal about moments you felt upset or overly emotional. Patterns will emerge, and you'll begin to map out your emotional trigger points. Think of it like being Sherlock Holmes, but for your feelings—elementary, my dear Watson!

Now, why do these specific things trigger you? It's usually not about the moment but something more profound. That snarky comment about your work may have reminded you of a hyper-critical teacher. Or your partner not texting back taps into deep-seated fears of being ignored or abandoned. Understanding the roots of your triggers—whether they stem from past experiences, insecurities, or unmet needs—helps you understand why your emotions might be going from naught to a hundred really quickly. It's like understanding the wiring behind a complicated control panel.

Once you've got a list of your triggers and understand their origins, it's time to map these triggers to your typical reactions. Do you shut down? Get angry? Withdraw? This mapping can illuminate your default settings and pave the way for tweaking your emotional responses. It's about recognizing that while you can't always control what triggers you, you can learn to control your reaction. This awareness is the first step toward not letting these triggers pull your emotional strings like you're a puppet in their dramatic play.

Practical Exercise: Trigger-Response Mapping

Grab a notebook or open a new document on your device and create two columns. In the first column, list the triggers you've identified. In the second, jot down how you typically react to each trigger. Next, think about how you'd instead respond. This simple exercise can help you visualize and plan better responses for the future.

Now, how about we get into some preventive strategies? Life will always throw you curveballs, so learning how to bat them is key. If you know certain situations or comments light your fuse, prepare for them. If it's a recurring situation (like those dreadful Monday meetings), rehearse calm responses beforehand. Visualization can be compelling here; imagine yourself handling the situation calmly and gracefully. Setting boundaries is also crucial. If specific topics are trigger mines, it's okay to communicate this to others and steer conversations away from these zones. And never underestimate the power of calming techniques like deep breathing or a quick walk to defuse anger or anxiety before it overwhelms you.

Handling emotional triggers is less about avoiding emotions and more about managing how they impact you and your social interactions. You can keep your emotional ship steady even in choppy waters by becoming more aware of your triggers, understanding their roots, and mapping out healthier responses. So next time you feel that familiar flare-up, remember: you have the tools to cool those embers.

EMOTIONAL REGULATION TECHNIQUES

So, you're in the middle of an intense, heat-packed argument, and suddenly, you feel like you're about to explode like a soda can that's been shaken too much. What do you do? You certainly don't want to erupt, spraying emotional debris everywhere. This is where emotional regulation techniques come into play, acting like that cool fridge that calms the soda down. These techniques are your secret arsenal for managing those bubbling emotions before they bubble over.

Let's kick things off with some immediate response strategies—because sometimes you need to cool things down, stat! When your emotions are skyrocketing, a few deep, deliberate breaths can be surprisingly powerful. It's not just an old wives' tale; it's about giving your body a mini reset. Deep breathing helps decrease your heart rate, signaling to your brain that it's time to chill out. Picture it as hitting the "cool" button on your internal thermostat. Another quick trick is counting—yes, just like you might count sheep to fall asleep. Count slowly to ten before you respond. It allows you to collect your thoughts and dilutes impulse reactions you might regret later.

Sensory awareness is another nifty trick. This involves grounding yourself by paying close attention to your senses. What can you see? What can you hear? It could be the clock ticking or the wallpaper's color. This helps pull your mind away from the emotional chaos and brings your focus to the present, reducing the intensity of the reaction.

Now, taming your emotions isn't just about putting out fires. It's also about building a robust, fire-resistant setup. That's where long-term emotional regulation strategies come into the picture. Regular mindfulness practice is like the gym for your emotional brain. Just as lifting weights builds muscle, regular mindfulness strengthens your mind's ability to stay calm and collected. It involves observing your thoughts and feelings without judgment, which, over time, can help you understand and manage your emotional responses better. Imagine your brain doing yoga—flexible, strong, and serene.

Cognitive restructuring is another long-term strategy worth adding to your emotional toolkit. It involves challenging and changing the distressing thoughts that often fuel emotional fires. For example, instead of thinking, "This is horrible; I can't handle it," you might reframe it as "This is challenging, but I can work through it." It's about tweaking your internal dialogue to be more supportive and less catastrophic.

Emotional journaling can also be a great way to process and regulate emotions. By writing down your feelings, you're effectively unpacking your emotional baggage, which can be incredibly therapeutic. It helps you to identify patterns in your emotional responses. It increases your self-awareness, making it easier to manage similar situations in the future.

But let's remember the role of physical health in all this. Ever noticed how a bad night's sleep or a junk food binge can leave you feeling emotionally fragile? That's because your physical health directly impacts your emotional stability. Adequate sleep, balanced nutrition, and regular exercise can significantly improve emotional regulation. Think of it like tuning an instrument; when your body is well-tuned, it can play through life's symphonies much more smoothly. Besides, no one likes being a grumpy bear because they skipped breakfast.

Applying these techniques in social settings is where you start seeing benefits. Imagine you're at a networking event, and a conversation turns toward a topic you're passionate about—not in a good way. Instead of letting your temper take the wheel, you tap into your emotional regulation toolkit. With a few deep breaths to steady your nerves and a moment of sensory awareness to ground yourself, you're ready to respond thoughtfully, keeping the conversation constructive instead of combative. These skills allow you to navigate social interactions with grace and poise, maintaining emotional balance even when the social seas get choppy.

Remember, managing your emotions isn't about suppressing them. It's about understanding, respecting, and ensuring they're expressed in healthy and constructive ways. With these techniques, you're well on your way to becoming a master of your emotional realm, capable of facing life's ups and downs with calm confidence. So next time you feel those emotional waves rising, remember your training and keep sailing smoothly forward.

EMPATHY IN ACTION: PRACTICAL SCENARIOS

Empathy isn't just about feeling warm and fuzzy; it's vital for navigating the rough seas of human emotions, turning potential storms into smooth sailing experiences. When you're faced with a tough conversation, maybe with a friend who's upset about losing their job or wrestling with a co-worker over a project gone awry, empathy is like the lifebuoy that keeps both of you afloat. It's about understanding where they're coming from, which can transform a clash into a dialogue and, who knows, lead to some unexpected solutions.

Picture this: You're in a heated discussion with a friend, feeling betrayed by someone else. Try dialing up your empathy instead of jumping in with advice or an opinion. Acknowledge their feelings with a simple, "That sounds really tough, and I can see why you're upset." This isn't just about making them feel heard; it's about validating their emotions without immediately trying to fix the problem. It shows you respect their feelings and are there to support them, not just solve problems. Plus, it saves you from the classic blunder of saying, "Well, at least ..." because nothing good ever follows those words.

Now, let's talk about empathy on a broader scale—like with people from different cultures, social backgrounds, or professional levels. Here's where empathy turns into a bit of an art form. It's about understanding that not everyone sees the world through your lens. A casual remark that's harmless to you might be offensive to someone from a different background. Dive into these interactions with an open mind and a hearty dose of curiosity. Ask questions, listen actively, and resist the urge to make assumptions. Remember, stereotypes are like fast food: easy to digest but not exactly good for understanding the rich flavors of diverse perspectives.

Role-playing exercises can be incredibly effective for honing your empathy skills. Grab a buddy and set up a scenario. One of you is a manager explaining a project delay to an upset client, or perhaps one of you is a tenant discussing a rent hike with a landlord. Take turns playing each role and discuss how it felt to be in each position. What did you notice about the other person's feelings? Was there a point where a bit more empathy could have changed the course of the conversation? This kind of practice can be eye-opening and is a safe way to make mistakes, learn from them, and improve.

Another powerful tool in your empathy toolkit is seeking feedback on how empathetic you come across in various situations. Reach out for feedback after a significant interaction, especially if it didn't go as smoothly as you'd hoped. Ask a trusted friend or a mentor, "How do you think I handled that? Was I empathetic enough? What could I have done differently?" This isn't about fishing for compliments or beating yourself up. It's about gaining insights that can fine-tune your approach next time. Adjust your behavior based on this feedback. You may need to work on keeping your emotions in check to remain more neutral, or you may need to practice listening more before jumping in with solutions.

Empathy, especially in action, is like a muscle—the more you use it, the stronger it gets. Empathy can elevate your social skills to new heights, whether you're dealing with a distressed friend, a diverse group of people, or just looking to improve your day-to-day interactions. It's about moving beyond just seeing to actually understanding, beyond hearing to genuinely listening. So, the next time you find yourself in a tricky social scenario, remember that a bit of empathy goes a long way.

BUILDING EMOTIONAL RESILIENCE

Ever felt like life was throwing dodgeballs at you, and no matter how nimble you were, one of them eventually hit you smack in the face? Well, that's where emotional resilience comes in handy. It's like having an invisible shield that helps you dodge, withstand, and even thrive amid those flying curveballs. Emotional resilience is your capacity to navigate through life's ups and downs without losing your groove. Whether it's a stressful day at work, a turbulent relationship, or the daily grind, resilience helps you bounce back stronger than ever.

Think of emotional resilience as your emotional immune system. Like a strong immune system keeps you healthy, a resilient mindset helps you maintain your emotional wellbeing. It's not about avoiding difficulties or emotions; it's about facing them head-on and emerging unscathed and improved. Resilience is built on self-awareness, understanding your emotional responses, and developing strategies to manage them. It involves seeing challenges not as insurmountable problems but as opportunities to learn and grow. Imagine you flub a presentation—instead of beating yourself up, you pivot to figuring out what went wrong, what you can learn, and how you can nail it next time. That's resilience in action. It's like being the MacGyver of your emotional toolkit, always ready to turn a paperclip and some duct tape into a solution.

Developing this resilient mindset isn't about flipping a magical switch. It's a skill that develops through conscious practice and attitude adjustments. Start by reframing how you view challenges. Instead of a 'Why me?' attitude, adopt a "Try me" stance. When you change your narrative from victim to victor, the challenges become less intimidating and more like puzzles to solve. Maintaining a long-term perspective also helps. This means looking beyond the immediate discomfort and focusing on long-term outcomes. It's like playing chess; sometimes, you've got to lose a pawn to win the game.

Now, no knight goes into battle alone, and neither should you. Building a robust support system is crucial for emotional resilience. This network, whether it's friends, family, or professional counselors, acts as your backup team. They provide perspectives, advice, and sometimes just the listening ear to process your emotions. Knowing when and how to lean on this support network is key. It's not about offloading your problems onto others but about engaging in a give-and-take that strengthens your emotional defenses.

Coping Strategies for Setbacks

When setbacks hit, and they will, having a toolkit of coping strategies makes all the difference. Start with maintaining motivation and optimism. This might sound like cheerleader fluff, but it's grounded in practicality. Setting small, achievable goals can keep your spirits and progress steady. Celebrate the little victories—yes, even something as simple as handling a stressful email well deserves a mental high five. These celebrations keep the momentum going and reinforce your resilience.

And what if the setback feels too big, like a boulder you can't push no matter how hard you try? That's when seeking professional help might be the best course of action. There's strength in recognizing when a situation is beyond your toolkit's repair capabilities. Therapists, counselors, or coaches can offer strategies and insights that are only sometimes apparent. They help you dissect the problem, understand your emotional response, and develop a tailored approach to tackling it.

Building and nurturing your emotional resilience is like constructing a dam; it needs regular maintenance, occasional reinforcement, and a good emergency plan. With resilience, you're better equipped to handle life's stresses without getting overwhelmed. You can face challenges with a grin (okay, maybe just a determined nod), knowing you've got the tools to deal with them. And as life throws those dodgeballs, you'll catch them—with style, no less—and throw them right back.

As we wrap up this chapter on building emotional resilience, remember: resilience isn't about never falling; it's about always getting back up. It's the secret ingredient that transforms life's trials into stepping stones, helping you navigate personal and professional landscapes with greater ease and confidence. Next, we'll explore how to apply these emotional tools in real-world scenarios, ensuring that you're surviving and thriving in your social world. So get ready to unleash your inner emotional ninja and tackle the world head-on!

CHAPTER 10
MAINTAINING SOCIAL SKILLS OVER TIME

Ah, the art of keeping your social skills not just alive but thriving—think of it as nurturing a garden of your favorite plants (or maybe that cactus you've miraculously not killed yet). Much like your green friends, social skills need continuous care and adaptation to flourish. Whether you're breezing through life changes like moving cities, starting a new job, or even sliding into retirement, each phase comes with its own social puzzles. Ready to become a social chameleon, adapting and growing through all of life's parties and potholes? Let's dig in!

LIFELONG SOCIAL SKILLS: ADAPTING AND GROWING

Recognizing Life Transitions

Life's a wild ride, and each new chapter—from launching a career to moving to a new neighborhood—shakes up your social landscape. These transitions can stir up a cocktail of excitement and anxiety, which, let's be honest, can make maintaining or forming new social connections feel like navigating a maze blindfolded.

The first step in managing this maze is recognizing that your social needs and skills are about to enter a new phase. It's like acknowledging the weather change; you wouldn't wear flip-flops in a snowstorm, right? Similarly, understanding that what worked socially in college (keg stands. anyone?) may not fly professionally is critical to adapting effectively.

Adapting Skills to New Contexts

So, you've recognized the change—excellent! Now, let's talk adaptation. Each new social setting is like stepping onto a new stage. The audience might be different, and your usual act might need some tweaking. Moving to a new city? Time to amp up those friend-making skills and perhaps adopt some local lingo or customs. Stepping into your first job? This might be the perfect moment to polish your small talk skills and learn the fine art of professional networking. The trick is to stay flexible and willing to learn from each new experience. Remember, social skills are not one size fits all; they're more like a tailored suit that needs adjustments to fit perfectly in different scenarios.

Continuous Learning and Openness

Keeping your social skills sharp is a lifelong quest like leveling up in a never-ending game of "Social Skills Warrior." This means staying curious and open to new methods of communication, especially in our fast-evolving digital world. Did everyone suddenly migrate from Facebook to some new app where messages disappear in a day? Time to get with the program! Keeping up with new communication technologies and cultural trends ensures you're not left behind using a fax machine in a Snapchat world. It's not just about keeping up—it's about staying engaged and relevant. No one wants to be that 48-year-old author who still talks about MySpace. By the way, I haven't done that in months.

Seeking Out New Social Opportunities

Now, for the fun part—putting all this learning into practice. Actively seeking new social opportunities is like sending out invites to your personal growth party. New in town? Maybe hit that local meet-up or community class. Newly retired? How about joining a club or volunteering? Each new interaction is a chance to test-drive your adapted and updated social skills. Plus, it's a fantastic way to enrich your social life and keep your emotional and mental health in tip-top shape. Who knows? The following person you meet at a pottery class might just become your next best friend or introduce you to a hobby that changes your life.

Embracing each life transition with the willingness to adapt your social skills, continuously learning from your experiences, and actively seeking new social scenarios doesn't just enhance your ability to connect with others; it enriches your entire life experience. As any good gardener knows, the key to vibrant growth is continual care, adaptation, and the courage to prune and adjust as needed. So, keep your social skills toolkit handy and your mind open; the world is your social oyster, ready to be explored and enjoyed.

TEACHING SOCIAL SKILLS TO OTHERS

When it comes to spreading the social skills cheer, think of yourself as the cool teacher everyone loved in school. Why? Because you've got the magic ingredient: role modeling. Like in those after-school specials, being a good role model isn't about being perfect; it's about showing how fundamental skills play out in the real world. Whether it's how you chat up the barista or negotiate peace treaties between squabbling friends, you're on display. Trust me: people are watching—learning how to handle praise gracefully, apologize when they mess up, or stay calm in a crisis just by observing you doing your thing.

Role modeling goes beyond just being polite. It's about demonstrating those juicy, complex social skills like empathy, conflict resolution, and even listening, like hearing the world's most fascinating story. It's one thing to tell someone to be empathetic but another to show them how you handle that co-worker who's always a bit (or a lot) on the grumpy side. This is your chance to show off how those skills can smooth out the daily grind and make life a bit brighter for everyone involved. Imagine yourself as the Mr. Miyagi of social finesse—wax on, wax off, empathy on, conflict off.

Now, let's chat about constructive feedback—because, let's face it, not everyone gets it right on the first go. Giving feedback is like being a coach: your job isn't to score goals but to help others play their best game. Start with the positives—what are they nailing already? From there, move on to the specifics, like, "Hey, I noticed during our chat you asked some awesome open-ended questions, but maybe next time, try to allow a bit more pause for the other person to respond." It's about guiding, not critiquing. Make your feedback the kind that fuels their desire to improve, not the kind that makes them want to throw in the towel.

Creating learning opportunities can be a blast. Think bigger than the traditional classroom—social skills flourish in the wild. Organize a group outing, a workshop, or a fun role-play session. Have you ever tried a "social scavenger hunt" where folks have to find someone who's been to Europe or who practices yoga? It's a fun way to break the ice and practice those introductions. Or how about a storytelling night where people share their most embarrassing or triumphant social moments? It's all about getting those social muscles to flex in a way that feels more like play and less like work.

Tailoring teaching methods to fit your audience is crucial. What works for a group of lively teenagers might not resonate with a room full of execs. Younger folks might dig a fast-paced, game-like workshop. At the same time, professionals might appreciate a more structured networking session with clear objectives. And remember, cultural and personal backgrounds greatly influence how people communicate. A deep dive into the nuances of body language might fascinate a globally diverse group and provide practical tips for international relations. Mixing up your methods keeps things fresh and respects the varied tapestry of human experiences. This isn't just teaching; it's an invitation to a grand social dance, and everyone has unique moves to contribute.

So, as you step into the role of a social skills sensei, remember that it's less about lecturing from the front and more about engaging with them in the thick of it. Show, don't just tell. Provide feedback that builds, not breaks. Create spaces that challenge and support, and be ready to switch up your style to meet them where they're at. Here's to being the role model who turns the mundane into magic, one interaction at a time.

REFLECTING ON SOCIAL GROWTH AND SETTING FUTURE GOALS

So, you've been working on your social skills and are starting to feel like you're getting the hang of this whole interaction thing. Great! But how do you keep this growth and not plateau like a forgotten New Year's resolution? It's time to get reflective and a bit strategic with your social prowess. Think of it as doing a little spring cleaning of your social skills closet—keeping what works, tossing what doesn't, and making room for new additions. Imagine you're Marie Kondo-ing your social life; if it doesn't spark joy, it's out!

Let's kick things off with some good old self-assessments. It's like taking a selfie, but you use your keen sense of self-awareness instead of a camera. Regularly taking stock of where you stand socially can be eye-opening. Start by asking yourself some simple questions: What social interactions have I handled well recently? Where did I feel most uncomfortable? This isn't about beating yourself up over your not-so-great chat last week. It's about gauging where you shine and where you could use a bit of polish. Reflect on the feedback you've received, both verbal and nonverbal. Maybe your friends enjoy your excellent listening skills, but you've noticed they glaze over when you dive into your deep love for 18th-century pottery. That's your cue: keep listening well but mix the conversation topics.

Now, let's talk goal setting—SMART goal setting, to be exact. Setting Specific, Measurable, Achievable, Relevant, and Time-bound goals isn't just for sales teams or fitness freaks; it's also gold for boosting your social skills. Say you want to get better at small talk because chatting about the weather or the latest sports scores at a party makes you want to run for the hills right now. A SMART goal might be, "I will initiate small talk with at least three people at the upcoming office party and engage each person for a minimum of five minutes." This goal isn't just a vague "get better at small talk" but a clear, actionable path you can realistically achieve and measure. And the best part? You get to tailor these goals to whatever social skills you want to develop.

Keeping a journal or log of your social interactions can be a game-changer. Think of it as your social diary, where you jot down what went well, what flopped, and how you felt about different interactions. Over time, this log will become a gold mine of insights, showing patterns in your interactions and tracking your progress. Did you find that talking about movies gets you more engaged responses than talking about your cat's dietary habits? That's valuable intel right there. Use your journal to plan how to steer future conversations toward more engaging topics or to strategize on improving areas that aren't going as well.

Lastly, remember to celebrate your social wins, no matter how small. Managed to chat with a new co-worker without awkward silences? That's a win. Did you keep cool during a heated group debate? Another win! Celebrating these victories keeps your morale high and motivates you to push your boundaries. And as you grow and evolve, so should your goals. You've nailed casual chitchat and are ready to tackle more profound, meaningful conversations. Adjust your goals accordingly, ensuring they continue to challenge and excite you.

As you wrap up this chapter on maintaining and advancing your social skills, remember that the key to continued growth is a mix of honest reflection, strategic goal setting, diligent tracking, and a healthy dose of celebration. Keep leaning into the learning, and soon, you'll see your social skills flourish and enjoy the process more than you ever thought possible. Ready to turn the page? Let's see what's next in your social skills saga!

CONCLUSION

Well, my friend, you've made it to the home stretch—the grand finale of our journey together through the lively world of social skills. We've traversed the terrain, from the basics of understanding and managing both our emotions and those of others to mastering the art of interaction across a spectrum of scenarios. From the foundational skills that get you through a casual chat at a coffee shop to the advanced finesse required in handling a high-stakes boardroom debate, it's been quite the ride, hasn't it?

Let's take a moment to recap some of the heavy hitters from our adventure: Emotional intelligence—the secret that keeps you tuned into your own emotional frequency and that of others. We've seen how pivotal empathy is as a nice-to-have and a cornerstone in building meaningful connections. Through conflict resolution, you've gained the tools to survive and thrive in the face of disagreements, turning potential battlefields into gardens of consensus. We've adapted these skills through various life transitions, highlighting the need for continuous learning and self-improvement—because, let's face it, social skills aren't a "set-it-and-forget-it" deal.

Enhancing your social skills is transformative, akin to upgrading your internal software to improve performance across all areas of life—personal relationships, professional success, and overall well-being. It's about making life not just livable but also enjoyable.

Now, here's where I nudge you gently but enthusiastically out of the nest. Take these strategies and insights and put them to work. Start small if you must—maybe strike up a conversation with a neighbor or finally address that long-standing conflict with a coworker. Observe, reflect, and marvel at how these changes positively impact your interactions. And if you find yourself tongue-tied, remember to take deep breaths and think of your funniest anecdote that doesn't involve bodily functions.

And hey, why keep all this newfound knowledge to yourself? Teach someone else the ropes. Whether helping a friend through a challenging conversation or coaching a team on effective communication, sharing your skills helps build a community of competent communicators. Plus, teaching is a fantastic way to deepen your own understanding. Who knew explaining the art of not oversharing could be so enlightening?

Remember, this book isn't a goodbye; it's a trusty companion on your social skills journey. I'm with you in spirit, cheering you on as you practice, stumble, learn, and eventually excel. Plus, I have more books coming to help you through your emotional intelligence journey. You've got this, and I'm proud to be a part of your toolkit.

Reflecting on my journey, I realize that mastering social skills has been both challenging and profoundly rewarding. I've had my share of awkward silences and foot-in-mouth moments. Still, each blunder was a stepping stone to better, more confident interactions. Your journey, too, will have its ups and downs, but the rewards are well worth the effort.

Thank you for taking this journey with me. I'm excited for you and all the wonderful, weird, and wide-ranging conversations you'll navigate with aplomb. Here's to your success in mastering social skills for a happier, more connected life. Go forth and communicate!

Cheers to your future,

Liam Grant

Now that you have everything you need to take control of your social interactions, it's time to pass on your newfound knowledge and show other readers where they can find the same help.

Your journey through "The Power of Connection" has equipped you with the tools to communicate effectively, build self-confidence, and foster meaningful relationships. You've learned to navigate social settings with ease, resolve conflicts constructively, and engage with empathy. Now, you have the power to help others discover these life-changing strategies too.

By leaving a review, you can:

- Help someone struggling to connect with others.
- Support a person seeking to improve their social skills and build stronger relationships.
- Encourage another reader to embark on their own journey of social growth and personal success.

Your review doesn't just reflect your thoughts—it becomes a beacon for others who are searching for guidance. It can inspire, motivate, and provide the reassurance that they are not alone in their quest for better social interactions and relationships.

So, if this book has made a difference in your life, please take a moment to share your experience. Your words could be the spark that someone else needs to start their transformation.

Simply scan the QR code below to leave your review:

Thank you for being part of this journey. Your insights and feedback mean the world to me and to countless others who will follow in your footsteps.

Your biggest fan,

Liam Grant

REFERENCES

1. Verywell Mind. (n.d.). Social anxiety coping skills: Best self-help strategies. https://www.verywellmind.com/coping-with-social-anxiety-disorder-3024836

2. Psychology Today. (n.d.). First impressions. https://www.psychologytoday.com/us/basics/first-impressions

3. HelpGuide. (n.d.). Body language and nonverbal communication. https://www.helpguide.org/articles/relationships-communication/nonverbal-communication.htm

4. Positive Psychology. (n.d.). Active listening: The art of empathetic conversation. https://positivepsychology.com/active-listening/

5. Fireflies.ai. (n.d.). 100+ conversation starters that work in any social setting. https://fireflies.ai/blog/conversation-starters/

6. PsychCentral. (n.d.). Mnemonic devices: Types, examples, and benefits. https://psychcentral.com/lib/memory-and-mnemonic-devices

7. Blinkist. (n.d.). Go beyond small talk: 24 conversation starters for 2024. https://www.blinkist.com/magazine/posts/go-beyond-small-talk

8. Science of People. (n.d.). Awkward silence: Make the most of it or get rid of it. https://www.scienceofpeople.com/awkward-silence/

9. BetterUp. (n.d.). Set social goals: 8 tips to get out there and make connections. https://www.betterup.com/blog/how-to-create-social-goals

10. Mayo Clinic. (n.d.). Fear of public speaking: How can I overcome it? https://www.mayoclinic.org/diseases-conditions/specific-phobias/expert-answers/fear-of-public-speaking/faq-20058416

11. American Psychological Association. (2012). The pain of social rejection. https://www.apa.org/monitor/2012/04/rejection

12. PsychCentral. (n.d.). How meditation can help you manage social anxiety. https://psychcentral.com/anxiety/how-meditation-can-help-you-manage-social-anxiety

13. Sales Odyssey. (n.d.). How to build an effective digital communication strategy. https://www.salesodyssey.com/blog/communication-strategy

14. Baylor University. (2024). More than just a smiley face: How emojis can affect communication. https://news.web.baylor.edu/news/story/2024/more-just-smiley-face-how-emojis-can-affect-communication

15. Google. (n.d.). Manage your online reputation. https://support.google.com/accounts/answer/1228138?hl=en

16. Harvard Business Review. (2020). 10 digital miscommunications — and how to avoid them. https://hbr.org/2020/03/10-digital-miscommunications-and-how-to-avoid-them

17. Influence at Work. (n.d.). Dr. Robert Cialdini's seven principles of persuasion. https://www.influenceatwork.com/7-principles-of-persuasion/

18. Program on Negotiation, Harvard University. (n.d.). Top 10 negotiation skills you must learn to succeed. https://www.pon.harvard.edu/daily/negotiation-skills-daily/top-10-negotiation-skills/

19. Test and Calc. (n.d.). Advanced empathy: The key to effective helping in mental health. https://testandcalc.com/richard/resources/Advanced%20Empathy.pdf

20. Management. (n.d.). Storytelling for personal and professional development. https://management.org/communicationskills/storytelling.htm

21. Indeed. (n.d.). 8 effective networking strategies for professionals. https://www.indeed.com/career-advice/career-development/networking-strategies

22. Brides. (n.d.). 50 first-date conversation topics and questions. https://www.brides.com/first-date-conversation-4177033

23. Body+Soul. (n.d.). How to prevent conflict at family gatherings. https://www.bodyandsoul.com.au/relationships/how-to-prevent-conflict-at-family-gatherings/news-story/45014a5575fedacf84442c3f67df71df

24. Day Translations. (n.d.). Cultural sensitivity in communication. https://www.daytranslations.com/blog/cultural-sensitivity-in-communication/

25. Positive Psychology. (n.d.). 7 ways to improve communication in relationships. https://positivepsychology.com/communication-in-relationships/

26. Persona Talent. (n.d.). How to build & maintain trust in professional relationships. https://www.personatalent.com/leadership-management/how-to-build-trust-in-professional-relationships/

27. Psychology Today. (2024). 9 proven ways to maintain a long-distance relationship. https://www.psychologytoday.com/us/blog/social-lights/202401/9-surefire-ways-to-nurture-a-long-distance-relationship

28. Shondaland. (n.d.). How to rekindle a friendship after years apart. https://www.shondaland.com/live/family/a38442412/how-to-rekindle-a-friendship-after-years-apart/

29. Wellable. (n.d.). 7 effective conflict resolution techniques in the workplace. https://www.wellable.co/blog/conflict-resolution-techniques-in-the-workplace/

30. Everyday Speech. (n.d.). Empathy: A cornerstone of effective communication and connection. https://everydayspeech.com/blog-posts/general/empathy-a-cornerstone-of-effective-communication-and-connection/

31. Verywell Mind. (2023). 6 de-escalation techniques to diffuse conflict. https://www.verywellmind.com/deescalation-techniques-to-diffuse-conflict-7498049

32. Manhattan CBT. (n.d.). Assertive vs. aggressive: What's the difference? https://manhattancbt.com/assertive-vs-aggressive/

33. RocheMartin. (n.d.). 4 of the best tools to measure and assess emotional intelligence. https://www.rochemartin.com/blog/best-tools-emotional-intelligence

34. BetterUp. (n.d.). Emotional triggers: What they are and 9 tips deal with them. https://www.betterup.com/blog/triggers

35. Greater Good Science Center, University of California, Berkeley. (n.d.). Five science-backed strategies to build resilience. https://greatergood.berkeley.edu/article/item/five_science_backed_strategies_to_build_resilience

36. Forward Counseling. (2023). Navigating change: Understanding the impact of life transitions. https://www.forwardcounseling.com/blog/2023/11/6/navigating-change-understanding-the-impact-of-life-transitions

37. Pumble. (n.d.). 18 business communication trends for 2024 and beyond. https://pumble.com/blog/communication-trends/

38. Everyday Speech. (n.d.). Teaching students to accept constructive criticism: A guide for educators. https://everydayspeech.com/blog-posts/general/teaching-students-to-accept-constructive-criticism-a-guide-for-educators/

39. Lifehack. (n.d.). 11 SMART goals examples for life improvement. https://www.lifehack.org/864427/examples-of-personal-smart-goals

ABOUT THE AUTHOR & UPCOMING PROJECTS

Liam Grant is a passionate writer and advocate for personal development and mental well-being. With over 20 years of experience in the insurance industry, Liam has honed his skills in communication, conflict resolution, and leadership—all of which he brings to his writing. His journey into the world of self-help and emotional intelligence began as a personal quest to better understand himself and others. This journey led him to write his first book, "Emotional Intelligence Unlocked," which has helped countless readers gain deeper insights into their emotions and improve their lives.

Liam's approachable, humorous style and genuine empathy for his readers make his books both relatable and impactful. When he's not writing or exploring new ideas for his next book, Liam enjoys spending time with his family in Boulder City, NV where he continues to find inspiration for his work.

Upcoming Projects:

Liam is excited to introduce his new series, "**The Power Series**", a collection of books dedicated to empowering readers to transform their lives. Each book in the series delves into a different aspect of personal growth, offering practical strategies and relatable stories to help readers thrive. The series will continue with "The Power of Emotions," where Liam shares techniques to master self-regulation including self-control and cultivating a balanced, fulfilling life.

Keep an eye out for upcoming titles in "The Power" series, including **"The Power of Anxiety-Free Living,"** **"The Power of Stress Management,"** **"The Power of Motivation,"** and many more. Each book promises to be a valuable guide, providing insights and tools to help you achieve your personal and professional goals—all while enjoying the journey.

Stay tuned for future releases in this empowering series, and join Liam on this exciting path to discovering your best self!